THE GAFFTA AWARDS

Larry Ryan is the editor of DangerHere.com and lives in Dublin, where he wears nothing but a sheepskin suit and gold-plated spotter's badge.

Gareth Power once made a net contribution to society. He now lives in semi-retirement, devoting his time exclusively to football quotes.

DangerHere.com's chief football writer Paul Little had a penchant for football guff from a very young age. Family legend has it that his first words were, 'I'm over the moon, Brian.'

FROM BECKS TO BIG RON – CELEBRATING THE
WONDERFUL WORLD OF FOOTBALL-SPEAK

THE GAFFTA

AWARDS

**Larry Ryan, Gareth Power
and Paul Little**

MAINSTREAM
PUBLISHING

EDINBURGH AND LONDON

Copyright © Larry Ryan, Gareth Power and Paul Little, 2004
All rights reserved
The moral rights of the authors have been asserted

First published in Great Britain in 2004 by
MAINSTREAM PUBLISHING COMPANY (EDINBURGH) LTD
7 Albany Street
Edinburgh EH1 3UG

ISBN 1 84018 922 3

A catalogue record for this book is
available from the British Library

Typeset in Badhouse and Van Djick
Printed and bound in Great Britain by
CPD Wales, Ebbw Vale

ACKNOWLEDGEMENTS

Spotter's badges to the rest of the Gaffta panel:

Ed Leahy
Phil Murray
Thomas Aherne
Jody Fitzpatrick
John Whelton

CONTENTS

INTRODUCTION

Let's face it, football-speak has taken over the world. We're all at it. Your boss won't consider a job well done unless you've given it '110 per cent'. You've only gone to work in the first place to 'earn your corn'. Yet when the bonuses are being handed out, you've 'seen them given for less'. Many a politician will begin a tirade about the health service with 'At the end of the day . . .' No deal is considered sealed 'until the fat lady sings'. And – admit it – in times of crisis, we all tend to 'take each day as it comes'.

A nameless contributor to this book once took things even further at a job interview: 'Well, I've come out of college and gone into telesales early doors.' Unsurprisingly, getting the job proved to be 'a big ask'.

That's only the tip of the iceberg. As football phrases creep into everyday language, the hard-working professionals inside the game are busy upping the ante ever further. Players, commentators, managers and pundits all have their contributions to make. Some devise their very own language; others craft outrageous metaphors; more simply visit atrocity upon the English language every time they open their mouths.

Do you know what Ron Atkinson means when he dismisses an ostensibly talented player as an 'amusement arcade'? Do you scratch your head when Ray Wilkins 'puts the hammer into Luton's coffin' or Kevin Keegan discovers 'a mole on the wall of the dressing-room'? Do you wince when you hear Glenn Hoddle encourage an injured player to 'do some running on his groin'?

Remember David Pleat telling us that 'for such a small man, Maradona gets great elevation on his balls'. How we laughed when Big Ron worried about the player who 'dribbles a lot and the opposition don't like it – you can see it all over their faces'. And fair play to sensitive beanpole Irishman Niall Quinn, who had kind words for the infertile referee who '. . . when he makes a decision, there's no arms thrown into the air and no gestating'.

There's plenty more of that kind of thing in this book, a definitive study of the timeless art of what we like to call 'guff' – a neat umbrella term for the lingo, gaffes and general foolishness so prevalent in football today. All of the game's leading 'guff merchants' are dissected. And along the way, we'll try to establish just what makes them tick.

We must remember, of course, that in today's dangerous world, no one is in more peril than the football talking head. It's not so long ago since Turkish pundit Ahmet Cakar was shot five times in the groin after repeatedly criticising local football officials. Fortunately, Cakar is alive and well enough to tell the tale, and he heroically refuses to be silenced. 'Bring them on,' he cried from a hospital bed. 'My flesh is thick!' What a man. Get this fella 20 minutes in a studio with Richard Keys and that's one pay-per-view event we wouldn't mind coughing up for.

The unfortunate incident only highlights the indefatigable courage and commitment of our noble guffsters, who fearlessly continue to chatter to camera and microphone daily, endlessly recycling their observations about this or that footballing matter.

What selfless reserves of human generosity gets these learned men to give weekly of their accumulated knowledge and experience in the face of such danger? 'A thousand notes a throw,' the cynics among you might suggest. But maybe there's more to it than that. OK, it's doubtful that Frank Stapleton would give you the time of day without some money changing hands, but what about the rest? Just what makes them do it? You can appreciate the professional commentators have to earn a crust, but what about the ex-footballers who now talk for a living? What are they playing at?

This book will try to find some answers. We know, for starters, that some are simply show-offs. Why would Ally McCoist or Rodney Marsh restrict the audience for their age-old routine of cast-off Kenneth Williams gags to a half-empty golf clubhouse in Marbella, when they can 'perform' for half of Britain every week instead?

While the likes of Big Ron – before he provided the biggest gaffe of all – seemed to have a genuine calling, others are simply going through the motions. Men like Gray, Hansen and Lawrenson are the McDonald's, Coca-Cola and Microsoft of punditry. You suspect they've long stopped caring where their ingredients come from or whether their source code is secure. When these boys step out of a studio for the last time, they'll never watch another game.

The rest are something of a rogues' gallery. A mixture of football's unemployed and unemployable. If you had a managerial track record like Chris Kamara's, you'd be only too happy to find a routine winner at the Stadium of Light pretty 'unnnnbelllllllievable', too.

Whatever the motivation, never has so much nonsense been said to so many by so few, and with such entertaining results. That's why we've decided it's time these brave few, this selfless breed of pundits, commentators, co-commentators, anchors, players, managers, radio hosts and general-purpose idiots are justly rewarded. And so, we have devised the Gaffta Awards. For the first time ever, these men (and Gabby Logan) will get the recognition they deserve – and some will even carry away our prestigious trophies, cast in the finest metaphorical gold.

There are 18 awards in total, celebrating all facets of the guff world. In each section, our panel of guffological experts have chosen a winner who, in their estimation, has simply produced the greatest quantity or quality of nonsense in that field.

Read the book from cover to cover, if you will. Or dive in and select an awards category, reading in sequence all about the also-rans, nominees and the winner. Or maybe you'd like to skip straight to one of your favourites? Perhaps take a lesson from the Word of Hod? Or find out where John Motson's commentaries usually come unstuck? We can tell you right now that Big Ron has earned a special award for Ronglish – his own personal dialect. An entire section is devoted to the basic vocabulary of this complicated language. See how many of his phrases you can slip in to your next job interview.

What with nobody buying pop singles any more, and today's movies invariably being rubbish, it's high time those discredited industries lost their monopoly on glamorous awards shindigs. As everyone knows, football punditry is the new rock 'n' roll. Roll out the red carpet. Let the Gafftas begin.

BEST GAFFER AWARD

THE GAFFTA AWARDS

Gérard Houllier once remarked that the most important time of a manager's working week was the post-match press conference. 'Especially when you're trying to deflect attention from your five-year plan's "phase of plateau",' the cynics among you suggest. For once, however, Le Scarf might well have a point.

With nobody bar Manchester United and Arsenal actually winning anything much, our judgements of Premiership managers are based almost entirely on their performances in front of the TV cameras. When David O'Leary was at Leeds, he annoyed the world with his weekly ravings about his babies and their fantastic adventures. In the end, he was laughed out of Elland Road for missing out on the Champions League. Now, since Dave has reinvented himself as a no-nonsense 'As I say, it's still just three points at the end of the day, as I say' man, he can miss out on the Big Cup for the Villa and still be hailed as a genius.

It's the same for all of them. Nobody ever noticed Gordon Strachan had lost six in seven as long as he cracked a few jokes for Geoff Shreeves. Steve McClaren keeps a hammock in a Sky outside-broadcast unit so often is he on the telly – and eventually it'll get him the England job. And they can finish round about the same positions in the table, but straight-talking David Moyes will be lauded to the rafters while we measure gaffoholic Kevin Keegan for a straitjacket.

And it's the likes of Kev who, for once, get their rewards in this section: The Gaffers. The men for whom the camera might not add six pounds but usually knocks about six hundred grand off their market value.

THE ALSO-RANS

☆Dave O'Leary
In a nutshell: Just a naive young Irishman learning his trade.
Gaffta Panel Verdict: The guff years peaked with *Leeds United on Trial*. Cleaned up act for Villa gig.

On his bottom-bunk relationship with Christophe Dugarry:
'I've never been an over-lover of his.'

On his mutually satisfying relationship with David Seaman:
'I'm a big lover of David.'

On a love affair with himself:
'I was shaking myself in many ways. I couldn't believe we were two goals down.'

On a job well done at Leeds:
'I like to breed players that attack people.'

☆Harry Redknapp
In a nutshell: The Del Boy of the guff game.
Gaffta Panel Verdict: Fine line in crafty cockney 'I'm the gaffer, innit' patter.

'Samassi Abou don't speak the English too good.'

'Dani is so good looking I don't know whether to play him or f*ck him.'

'Where are we in relation to Europe? Not far from Dover.'

'With the foreign players, it's more difficult. Most of them don't even bother with the golf, they don't want to go racing. They don't even drink.'

☆Dave 'Harry' Bassett
In a nutshell: The man that never stayed sacked.
Gaffta Panel Verdict: Has made as many gaffes as he's had clubs relegated.

'You have got to miss them to score sometimes.'

'It's been two ends of the same coin.'

'And I honestly believe we can go all the way to Wembley unless somebody knocks us out.'

'It would be foolish to believe that automatic promotion is automatic in any way whatsoever.'

☆Barry Fry
In a nutshell: If trophies were awarded for self-publicity, Bazza would be Marcello Lippi.
Gaffta Panel Verdict: Guff aplenty, but give him an award and it'll be open season for gaffers to urinate on corner flags!

'Tony Adams was a born winner from a very young age.'

On the Man United team of the '60s:
'On the field they got on great; off the field they didn't social much.'

☆Gérard Houllier

In a nutshell: Excuse-making, hide-covering scarf sporter.
Gaffta Panel Verdict: Never really turned the guff corner.

'You cannot say my team aren't winners. They've proved that by finishing fourth, third and second in the last three years.'

On Fergie:
'A work alcoholic.'

☆Bobby Gould

In a nutshell: Veteran beneficiary of eternal managerial merry-go-round.
Gaffta Panel Verdict: As good a public speaker as he was a Wales manager.

'We are really lucky this year because Christmas falls on Christmas Day.'

'Arsenal are passing it so quickly. Full marks to them. They must work on it at training.'

'The back four played their way out with lovely triangles.'

☆Arsène Wenger

In a nutshell: *Le Prof qui n'est pas vu.*
Gaffta Panel Verdict: Has his moments, but probably spouts most of his guff as a football 'consultant' for French television.

'If you buy a man who is half-dead, everybody may be happy off the field, but on the field you'll have major problems.'

'My players all have different strong points. Thierry Henry has power and pace nobody else has. Davor Suker has a left leg and a nose in the box.'

'I know you're going to laugh, but I didn't see the incident.'

On a Sol Campbell suspension:
'This is farcical. We must be living in farci-land.'

☆Brian Clough
In a nutshell: The ghost of guffness past.
Gaffta Panel Verdict: Showed the current crop the way. Gordon Strachan's post-match interview role model.

'Brazil, the favourites – if they are the favourites, which they are.'

After hearing of Souness's heart surgery:
'My heart goes out to Graeme Souness.'

☆Steve Coppell
In a nutshell: Crocked winger turned young manager with promise. Destined to be remembered as a crocked winger.
Gaffta Panel Verdict: Management highlights pre-Sky Sports – hasn't adapted well to mass footie coverage.

'He's carrying his left leg, which, to be honest, is his only leg.'

'I'm not going to make it a target, but it's something to aim for.'

'At the end of the day, it's all about what's on the shelf at the end of the year.'

THE NOMINEES

☆Glenn Hoddle

In a nutshell: Spiritual gaffer persecuted for his beliefs.

Gaffta Panel Verdict: In need of a second coming to get the show on the road once more. Out of the action too long to get a gong.

Misunderstood genius, entertainer, advertiser, seer, guru, leader of men, sporter of complicated haircuts. These things and many more has Glenn Hoddle been during the meteoric blaze across the heavens that has been his career to date.

It all began in the early 1980s when Glenn, a precocious teenage practitioner of silky skills, established himself as a Spurs and England star. His talent was prodigious, as indeed was his mullet. Adored by millions, Glenn had the world at his feet, so to speak.

Famously long and tanned of leg, ladies everywhere swooned as he sported the very shorts Kylie used to launch her pop comeback. It seemed as though things could not get much better, and yet that is exactly what they did in 1987 when 'Diamond Lights', the synth-pop masterpiece he recorded with mate Chris Waddle, stormed up the hit parade. As if that was not enough, Glenn proved himself a dab hand as a thespian in the early 1990s when he lined out in a TV ad with his kids and then-wife to tout the virtues of breakfast cereal Shredded Wheat.

And still Glenn was not content. For him, all this material success counted for nothing unless backed up by some kind of spiritual dimension. That was where Jesus-like 'healer' Eileen Drewery came in. Not only did she offer Ray Parlour the option of a quick short-back-and-sides but Eileen also provided Glenn with access to the divine, and with it some handy tips on how to run a football team.

With her by his side, Glenn might not have overseen much heavenly football, but his managerial doctrine drew heavily on theological insight – 'The Word of Hod', some called it. Look at what happened, for example, when one of his disciples (Darren Anderton, most likely) fell victim to a heavy challenge.

Hoddle had known all along that the two-footed lunge had been written in scripture:

'His tackle was definitely pre-ordained.'

Of course, when you've got powers like Hod, you tend to assume that others have been just as favourably treated by the man upstairs. Omnipresence, for instance, is taken for granted:

'They were still in the dressing-room when they came out for the second half.'

Strangely, for a religious sort, Hod didn't seem to have much truck with Jesus, considering him a John the Baptist-like figure who merely prefigured the true Resurrection, which occurred during a half-time team talk at White Hart Lane:

'We threw caution to the wind and came back from the dead. Well, it is Easter Monday.'

In fact, if Jesus was around today, it looks like he'd have a job on his hands grabbing the number 9 shirt from Drewery in any Hoddle set-up:

'Look at Jesus. He was a normal run-of-the-mill sort of guy who had a genuine gift, just as Eileen has.'

The real problems started, however, when Hoddle began to preach. Luckily, this reading fell on deaf (and baffled) ears:

'In this moment in time, if that changes in years to come I don't know, but what happens here today and changes as we go along that is part of life's learning and part of your inner beliefs.'

But Glenn's temple came crashing down when he seemed to suggest that the disabled were being made to pay for sins in a previous life. Naturally, he immediately voiced an eloquent denial of the accusations:

'At this moment in time, I never said them things about those people.'

To no avail, however, and, ironically, it was Glenn who paid a heavy price for his sins as he was given the sack from the England job.

Needless to say, you cannot keep a good man down. And a respected coach with the tactical insight Glenn had shown would not be out of work for long. So shrewd was Glenn on the training ground that it seemed some of his sides had an extra man on the pitch:

'We changed to a back four and went 4–4–3 and after that 20-minute period we grew in our game.'

Nor has any player of Glenn's ever gone out unsure about the official duration of the match:

'Football's all about 90 minutes.'

And Hod gets little or no recognition for a discovery that every player and coach nowadays takes for granted:

'When a player gets to 30, so does his body.'

While he was with England, Hoddle had devised a fail-safe master plan for dealing with the likes of Argentina:

'I think in international football you have to be able to handle the ball.'

And it was innovative, though admittedly painful, rehabilitation programmes like this that helped Hoddle work his way through Tottenham's sick notes:

'Robert Lee was able to do some running on his groin for the first time.'

But it's not all about footballing nous for Glenn. Sometimes the power of his words alone is enough to inspire a man to go out and play like Pelé:

'They needed a leadership on the pitch. And do your disciplines on the post and we could have won.'

He can even inspire some of those past-life sinners to do a job for him:

'He was a player that hasn't had to use his legs even when he was nineteen years of age because his first two yards were in his head.'

His command of the English language really is second to none:

'Arsenal have got over their blimp.'

'Ilie has a deception of pace.'

'International football is one clog further up the football ladder.'

Of course, a great theological mind like Glenn's is always likely to be a great philosophical mind too:

'It's not a night for this or that.'

Nor indeed for these or those.

'I have a number of alternatives, and each one gives me something different.'

The kind of alternatives we'd all like to have.

'Seventy-five per cent of what happens to Paul Gascoigne in his life is fiction.'

Minder Jimmy Five Bellies must fervently wish that those infamous Gazza torture sessions were among the fictional bits.

'With hindsight, it's easy to look at it with hindsight.'
Only Glenn had the foresight to see this.

All in all, it's difficult to see how this inspirational leader of men has ever found himself without gainful employment. Perhaps, as he might say himself:
'We didn't have the run of the mill.'

☆Kevin Keegan

In a nutshell: Football's eternal optimist – who's being ground down unceasingly by football reality.
Gaffta Panel Verdict: Pushed the winner hard, but the panel decided not to give him the award to keep him hungry. We don't want Keegan retiring to the golf course just yet!

Who said this, apropos of transfer windows?
'Well, that's like asking me who is on my Christmas card list. I sit down with the wife and I say, "Did they send us one last year or this year?", and if they haven't, we rip the name up and throw it in the bin. But then, a couple of days after Christmas, the card might arrive late so we do a card for them on the 28th and date it the 22nd and send it off and hope they don't notice . . . I haven't a clue what I'm talking about.'
Who else? None other than guff immortal Kevin Keegan. Many have stepped up to the nonsense plate, but no one has ever spouted more out-and-out gibberish than Kev. And it's not just in the guff stakes that he has provided entertainment over the decades. There are also his 1970s 'hit' singles 'Head Over Heels In Love' and 'It Ain't Easy', not to mention his spectacular bicycle crash on *Superstars*. Two European Footballer of the Year awards pale in comparison with such achievements.

Kev's teams play the way he talks – rushing headlong into trouble without ever considering the bothersome issue of whether what they are at is actually sensible. It's often bloomin' entertaining, though. We would 'luv it' if Kev keeps on doing what he's doing for many years to come.

And so, we give you the full glory of the wit and wisdom of Kevin Keegan.

KEV AND PLAYERS:

'The substitute is about to come on – he's a player who was left out of the starting line-up today.'
ITV pay big money for this kind of incisive analysis.

'I don't think there's anyone bigger or smaller than Maradona.'
Surely you can think of someone.

'Despite his white boots, he has real pace.'
Give him a black pair and he'd be uncatchable.

'The 33 or 34 year olds will be 36 or 37 by the time the next World Cup comes around, if they're not careful.'
Because if you let your age go, it's very difficult to reduce it again.

'He's using his strength. And that is his strength – his strength.'
Strong words.

'Nicolas Anelka left Arsenal for £23 million and they built a training ground on him.'
Understandable actions by Arsenal, in the circumstances, but Nick managed to dig himself back out.

'They compare Steve McManaman to Steve Heighway and he's nothing like him, but I can see why – it's because he's a bit different.'
Reminiscent of the old Frank Carson joke – 'What's the difference between a duck?'

'I would ask anyone to try to understand the world he lives in. We all have to accept that he is married to Spice Girl Victoria Adams – and I think he copes very well with it.'
A touching appeal for compassion for unfortunate David Beckham.

'Goalkeepers aren't born today until they're in their late 20s or 30s.'
The labour pains must be terrible.

'You can't play with a one-armed goalkeeper . . . not at this level.'
Maybe in Scotland.

'The last thing I wrote on the board before we came out was: "If you go out there and show me that determination and you show this crowd that you want it more, they'll be that 12th man for you. They'll give you that extra lift."'
It was half-time before they reached the pitch.

KEV AND THE OBVIOUS:
'There'll be no siestas in Madrid tonight.'
A safe enough bet.

'Argentina won't be at Euro 2000 because they're from South America.'
Hard to argue.

KEV AND POST-MORTEMS:
'At this level, if five or six of you don't turn up, you'll get beat.'
Better have a roll-call on the bus then.

'You just need one or two players playing well to have a chance in this league. But you need nine or ten playing well to have a chance to win.'
You just need one Kevin Keegan to have a chance of guff.

'We don't get any marks for effort like in ice-skating.'
Should we break it to Kev that hapless endeavour goes just as unrewarded on the rink?

'I'm not trying to make excuses, but I think the lights may have been a problem.'
Kev makes excuses for David Seaman's latest howler.

'You can't do better than go away from home and get a draw.'
Might help explain Manchester City's poor away form . . .

KEV AND CONTRADICTIONS:
'Richard Dunne has always been in the frame for me. When he has been out of the frame, it was because he took himself out of it for one reason or another.'
One of those reasons may have had something to do with Dunner's ample frame.

'Gary always weighed up his options, especially when he had no choice.'
Kev should have weighed up his options before he said this.

And speaking of options:
'Chile have three options – they could win or they could lose.'

'England have the best fans in the world, and Scotland's fans are second-to-none.'
Bet-hedging of which Trevor Brooking would be proud.

'I came to Nantes two years ago and it's much the same today, except that it's completely different.'
And to think the sentence had started so brightly with the promise of cultural insight.

KEV AND . . . KEV-NESS:

'Hungary is very similar to Bulgaria. I know they're different countries . . .'
Do you, Kev? Do you really?

'In some ways, cramp is worse than having a broken leg.'
Clearly, Keggy has never had a broken leg.

'I know what is around the corner – I just don't know where the corner is.'
Profound in its own way, we reckon.

'It's understandable that people are keeping one eye on the pot and another up the chimney.'
Understandable is not a word we'd associate with this remark.

'I'd love to be a mole on the wall in the dressing-room.'
A mole with climbing gear, presumably.

'The tide is very much in our court now.'
Should probably talk to the groundskeeper about that.

'I've had an interest in racing all my life, or longer really.'
Kev and Hod often get together to discuss their past lives.

'England can end the millennium as it started – as the greatest football nation in the world.'
Perhaps it was in a past life that Kev learned so much about eleventh-century football.

'Life wouldn't be worth living if you could buy confidence, because the rich people would have it all and everybody else would . . . would have to make their own arrangements.'
Kev has already made his own arrangements in the making-sense department.

☆Ian Holloway

In a nutshell: Up-and-coming guff star with penchant for lad culture.

Gaffta Panel Verdict: Has produced magic, but needs to let the guff flow spontaneously from within. The panel suspects he's started using pre-prepared lines!

QPR manager Ian Holloway is a rising star of football guffland. He may have been bossing down the divisions of late, but recent performances suggest he may be Premiership class when it comes to the quotable quote and the soundable soundbite. With precious few managers in the lower reaches with any kind of profile, Holloway seems destined for stardom. Good manager or not, he may just blag his way to the top. For now, he looks set to replace Barry Fry as the standard-bearer for those who reside outside of the Premiership spotlight.

Holloway's style revolves around the quest for the perfect soundbite. In season 2003–04, he hit the jackpot after his side's grim away win at Chesterfield – his cracking laddish metaphor for winning ugly catapulted him to the nation's attention:

'To put it in gentleman's terms, if you've been out for a night and you're looking for a young lady and you pull one, some weeks they're good looking and some weeks they're not the best. Our performance today would have been not the best-looking bird, but at least we got her in the taxi. She weren't the best-looking lady we ended up taking home, but she was very pleasant and very nice, so thanks very much let's have a coffee.'

And with that, the die was cast. Quote collectors now point their sharpened pencils in his direction – and Holloway has been only too happy to oblige.

On a denied penalty at Grimsby, Holloway summoned his wife:

'Everyone was laughing because if that was not a penalty, then what was? I think my wife even saw that and she's down in St Albans listening to the radio!'

Holloway threw down the gauntlet to the boo boys at Loftus Road:

'Most of our fans get behind us and are fantastic, but those who don't should shut the hell up or they can come round to my house and I will fight them.'

On winding down, Holloway finds a unique form of therapy:

'I've had a week from hell; I'm trying to learn how to relax. I'm now going to enjoy this, take my brain out and stick it in an ice bucket.'

On winning the promotion race, Holloway took it by a nose:

'If you can keep your noses in front at the end, that's what counts. It's been said that I have a bit of a Roman nose, and I am keeping it ahead at the moment. Hopefully it's all about the length of your hooter because I might be in front at the end of the season as well.'

On running the Rs, Holloway goes all Will Smith:

'It's like the film *Men in Black*. I walk around in a black suit, white shirt and black tie . . . I've had to flash my white light every now and again to erase some memories, but I feel we've got hold of the galaxy now . . . it's in our hands.'

And when it comes to counting chickens, Holloway knows how to avoid being sick as a parrot:

'I used to keep parakeets, and I never counted every egg thinking I would get all eight birds – you just hoped they came out of the nest box looking all right.'

No doubt there's much more to come – there may even be a book in it. But it's early doors for Holloway – and let's hope this young manager doesn't get blinded by the limelight. Already, it's become unclear whether Holloway prefers press conferences to football. But post-match press sessions at Loftus Road are frankly small beer. Holloway would do well to remember that football has to be much more than just a means to an end. If he's to reach the heady heights of, say, a Ron Atkinson, success on the pitch (promotion to the Premiership and a cup or two) is required before he gets the kind of national exposure for his talents that a slot on a terrestrial channel's football panel can bring.

That said, perhaps an alternative route to football-speak stardom lies on Sky Sports. Maybe a period in the reserves with the likes of Claridge and Aldridge on Tuesday and Wednesday Worthington Cup nights could eventually earn him a prestigious slot beside Stelling on Saturday. But this is a precarious and cut-throat career path – the likes of Clive Allen and Tony Cottee will not just hand over their headsets and swivel chairs to anyone. Success will demand Holloway's full attention – the Rs job would have to go – if the Bristol man is to prove that he is indeed all talk.

☆Gordon Strachan

In a nutshell: The one man who has turned post-match guff to his own advantage.
Gaffta Panel Verdict: A contender, but intentional humour is no substitute for the real thing.

Ensuring you get an easy ride from football reporters in ten easy steps:

1. Welcome to Southampton Football Club. Do you think you are the right man to turn things around?
'No! I was asked if I thought I was the right man for the job

and I said, "No, I think they should have got George Graham because I'm useless!"'

2. Is that your best start to a season?
'Well, I've still got a job so it's far better than the Coventry one, that's for sure.'

3. Are you getting where you want to be with this team?
'We're not doing bad. What do you expect us to be like? We were eighth in the league last year, in the Cup final and we got into Europe. I don't know where you expect me to get to. Do you expect us to win the Champions League?'

4. Gordon, you must be delighted with that result?
'You're spot on! You can read me like a book.'

5. What about Augustin Delgado?
'I've got more important things to think about. I've got a yoghurt to finish by today, the expiry date is today. That can be my priority rather than Augustin Delgado.'

6. This might sound like a daft question, but you'll be happy to get your first win under your belt, won't you?
'You're right. It is a daft question. I'm not even going to bother answering that one. It is a daft question, you're spot on there.'

7. Bang, there goes your unbeaten run. Can you take it?
'No, I'm just going to crumble like a wreck. I'll go home, become an alcoholic and maybe jump off a bridge. Umm, I think I can take it, yeah.'

8. There's no negative vibes or negative feelings here?
'Apart from yourself, we're all quite positive round here. I'm going to whack you over the head with a big stick, down, negative man, down.'

9. Marian Pahars: is he fit?

'He's caught every virus going except a computer virus, and he is probably working on that even now.'

10. You don't take losing lightly, do you, Gordon?

'I don't take stupid comments lightly either.'

☆ Howard Wilkinson

In a nutshell: The man who thought he could learn footie from a book.

Gaffta Panel Verdict: Sensational spurts of guff, but needs full-time employment at the sharp end to gain the necessary level of consistency.

Now here's a clever man: look, he's covered head to toe in UEFA coaching badges! What a smart fellow! But hang on a second – doesn't Ian Rush have those badges as well? Hmmm . . . maybe this man isn't the football genius he'd love us to think he is. No, in fact, he definitely isn't. Why? Because it's none other than barmy old Howard Wilkinson! Dear old Howard – living proof that for football managers, qualifications alone do not maketh the man. Deep down, how disappointed he must be with the results of all that study – in his heart of hearts, he knows he may as well have stuck with Charles Hughes' mythical FA coaching manual. Qualifications don't add up to a hill of beans when you're inherently rubbish at managing football teams.

But while Wilko's star has faded in the firmament of the footie manager, his place is assured in the honour roll of football guff practitioners. In fact, after years on the sidelines – working as the FA's Technical Director – Wilkinson proved his enduring greatness by getting the public to laugh at him, rather than at his dire Sunderland team. Magic.

As a purveyor of football nonsense, Wilko specialises in David Brent-like homespun philosophy, mathematical mastery, self-delusion and the bizarre.

PHILOSOPHY:

Elucidating on his playing staff at the Stadium of Light, Wilko threw us this pearl of wisdom:

'Our squad looks good on paper. But paper teams win paper cups.'

The Sunderland months will also be remembered for an insight into the complex world of recruitment – one that has surely found its way into business text books everywhere:

'If you hire people who are smarter than you, maybe you are showing that you are a little bit smarter than them.'

Ricky Gervais was no doubt tied up for weeks in negotiations with Wilko's people trying to buy the rights to use the line in the US version of *The Office*.

THE NUMBERS GAME:

With the Mackems languishing at the foot of the table, Wilko was famously asked by Garth Crooks on *Football Focus* whether he felt there were three worse teams in the Premiership than Sunderland. Wilko's reply was masterly:

'I'm not concerned if we are one of the three worst, I want us to be the fourth-best down there.'

Leaving Sunderland, Wilko was rightly proud of easily achieving his goal.

In fairness to the lad, he eventually insisted on adding a sums module to one of those courses of his. The improvement was immediate:

'I'm a firm believer that if the other side scores first you have to score twice to win.'

SELF-DELUSION:

'I would say relegation is three from four because we are already out of it in my mind. When I look at our fixtures, thankfully they are against teams around us, which makes

them better fixtures. I believe we are going to get out of it and I am not too bothered who else is going to get out of it. I don't have to think about what relegation would mean to this club because I have been in the business a long time.'

Howard showing that he was from the 'ignore it and it'll go away' school of football management. Howard ignored the relegation dogfight and Sunderland went away.

After just a few weeks at Sunderland, it appears that Wilko had something of an epiphany:

'Jesus Christ couldn't come in here with a system that would cure the way we have been playing.'

Especially as the Good Lord himself doesn't have the coaching badges.

Eventually it all became too much for Howard:

'It's like trying to push custard up a hill!'

THE BIZARRE:

After a depressing 4–1 drubbing by Spurs and a memorably bad-tempered press conference, an under-the-weather Wilko admitted:

'[It's] not easy to sit here with a temperature and a thumping head and be belle of the ball and play the tambourine.'

Yorkshire balls are obviously unusual affairs.

There would, however, be no cover-up. Or something . . .

'We are not putting our cape over the tunnel; we are putting our cape in the tunnel.'

The real benefit of Wilko's qualifications can be seen in his colourful analyses of other great figures in the game:

'Zinedine Zidane could be a champion sumo wrestler. He can run like a crab or a gazelle.'

Yes, Wilko deserves his place in the pantheon of the greats. With luck – and perhaps boosted by his Gaffta nomination – Wilko will, sooner or later, guff his way into another high-profile post. The man surely has so much more to offer.

☆Bryan Robson

In a nutshell: Revered England captain who dilutes his reputation with every managerial post.

Gaffta Panel Verdict: Sliding into managerial obscurity, a move to full-time punditry could provide an income and a proper chance of Gaffta glory next time round.

Legendary midfielder Bryan Robson could hardly put a foot wrong as a player. His managerial career has to date been somewhat less impressive. Thankfully, he's compensated by being a solid, dependable generator of football guff, whether . . .

AS A PUNDIT:

'The pressure's on Arsenal to win their games. And now they've got to score goals as well to win those games.'
You don't say, Bryan?

'The penalty decisions were brought in to punish those teams that gave them away.'
This revelation rocked the world of football when Robbo leaked it to the media.

'Danny Murphy's been scoring with benders all season.'
Now this is more interesting. The tabloids will pay Robbo a fortune for this kind of information.

'Paolo Di Canio is capable of scoring the goal he scored.'
Someone should let Di Canio know. Then he'd go and score one of those goals.

OR AS A HAPLESS GAFFER:

'If we played like this every week, we wouldn't be so inconsistent.'

At least he's consistent in the nonsense league.

'It wasn't going to be our day on the night.'

Was always a faint hope, let's be realistic.

'We're going to start the game at 0–0 and go out and try to get some goals.'

The secret of his managerial success.

'It's a bit easier after that win over Newcastle. That's a result that takes us that little bit further from safety.'

Perhaps explains how he successfully achieved relegation with Middlesbrough.

☆ Jack Charlton

In a nutshell: World Cup winner, Leeds stalwart and professional angler who dragged international football down to his level with Ireland.

Gaffta Panel Verdict: A genuine contender, but needs to spend more time on the airwaves than in waders.

Big Jack's done it all – won the World Cup, starred in a great Leeds side, led the Republic of Ireland to unprecedented success as a manager. But these days he's left all that behind. Now most of his time is spent fishing or otherwise relaxing. Some would say that this is not much different to when he was a 'working' man. Certainly, his decade as Ireland manager was a leisurely time. Some would say he was a bit too laid back in those days:

'If in winning we only draw, we would be fine.'

Not for Jack, research about the opposition:

'We probably got on better with the likes of Holland,

Belgium, Norway and Sweden, some of whom are not even European.'

Or even about his own squad:
'He's a great little player . . . who scored it again?'

He gives it an impossibly full gun keeping up with the latest football news:
'I've seen them on television on a Sunday morning most days of the week.'

His post-mortems when things went wrong were a bit iffy:
'It was a game we should have won. We lost it because we thought we were going to win it. But then again, I thought that there was no way we were going to get a result there.'

As a pundit, Jack was rather less than assured:
'The Arsenal defence is skating close to the wind.'

'It was a definite penalty but Wright made a right swansong of it.'

But the most worrying Big Jack trait is surely his tendency to risk provoking outrage. His status as living saint in Ireland was put in jeopardy when he expressed less than enthusiastic sentiment about the traditional Irish game hurling:
'I'm always suspicious of games where you're the only ones that play it.'

☆Claudio Ranieri

In a nutshell: Genial Roman who could melt even the hardest heart.

Gaffta Panel Verdict: Language barrier might explain much of the guff – an unfair advantage that the committee could not overlook.

He came, he saw, he tinkered. Those who ultimately saw Claudio Ranieri's reign as Chelsea manager as being a failure haven't looked beyond the second-place Premiership finish and tame European exit to see the extraordinary work the genial Roman was doing behind the scenes.

Of course trophies are nice to have, but posterity will never forget how Claudio used his time at Stamford Bridge to compile the first ever Anglo-Italian guff phrasebook. Here's just some of the handy phrases Claudio and his magnificent team of language tutors have prepared for future generations of English-based Italian gaffers.

It's important to retain a sizeable squad:
'If it is the case that you need just a first eleven and three or four more players, then why did Christopher Columbus sail to India to discover America?'

Maybe I shouldn't have brought on Seba Veron:
'Football managers are like a parachutist. At times it doesn't open. Here, it is an umbrella. You understand, Mary Poppins?'

I won't tolerate interference with team selection:
'Damien is Damien. When I don't put him in the squad, my mother, who's 84, asks "Why isn't Damien playing?" She kills me about it and that's true.'

Good evening, gentlemen of the press:
'Hello, sharks.'

Those Arsenal lads are a lively bunch, aren't they?
'They showed good stamina and good vitamins.'

I'm about to get the sack, so I'll just talk rubbish to distract you for a while:
'Before you kill me, you call me the "dead man walking". I must buy you an espresso. But only a little one – I am Scottish.'

If only that Russian guy would leave me alone:
'I am happy when our fans are happy, when our players are happy and our chairman is on the moon.'

I'm a big fan of David O'Leary's coaching methods:
'It is my baby. Maybe soon it will be ready to get out of the pram . . . I will lead it by the hand.'

I've been learning English from my five year old's A to Z of Animals*:*
'I once said Jimmy Floyd Hasselbaink is like a shark and Carlton Cole like a lion. Well, Adrian Mutu is another born predator. In fact, Mutu is like a snake.'

What diverse coaching techniques we use:
'One coach was training a player's hair, and another was training another part of his body.'

I wish someone else would pick the bloody team because I haven't a clue:
'Having so many great players at my disposal is bringing out the best in me. I feel like a chef because, with good ingredients, you can cook anything, the most fantastic dinner. One day, I hope to become the Gordon Ramsay of football. But, at the moment, that title still belongs to Alex Ferguson. I only have one Michelin star and he has three.'

Doh!
'I can't change now. I'm like Frank Sinatra – I always do it my way. I told the players everything I did in the Monaco game was wrong. I changed things to win the match – but we lost and I was thinking, "Oh f***, Claudio, why, why? Bad Tinkerman!"'

WINNER

☆Bobby Robson

In a nutshell: Dazed, confused and bewildered – but still in love with football.

Gaffta Panel Verdict: Think of Paul Newman finally winning an Oscar for *The Colour of Money*.

Probably the only current football manager to have lived through the industrial revolution – some even suggest he invented the Spinning Jenny – avuncular Bobby Robson is the grand old man of football. Not for him the path beaten by the likes of Bobby Charlton, who tours the world Queen Mother-like, paying goodwill visits to places like Bermuda and Dubai. Septuagenarian Bobby is made of sterner stuff than that, remaining involved in football at its highest level. That he is also still producing guff at the highest level simply makes us admire him all the more.

Bobby's a dab hand at the effective metaphor, the image that makes a complex concept clear as a bell:

'We put some good subs on to hang onto the fort.'

'Tottenham have impressed me – they haven't thrown in the towel even though they've been under the gun.'

'When Gazza was dribbling, he used to go through a minefield with his arm, a bit like you go through a supermarket.'

It's not widely appreciated that he's the Cassius Clay of modern times. Who else in the world of sport can compose an amusing poetic ditty off the cuff?

'We've voodooed the hoodoo!'

'We need to get that point as soon as possible. The tooter the sweeter.'

A particular speciality of Bobby's is the contradiction. He has that rare ability to begin a sentence with an utterance that, by the time the sentence stumbles to its conclusion, has been comprehensively gainsaid. Evidence for the prosecution, m'lud:

'Manchester United dropped points, Liverpool dropped points, Chelsea dropped points, Everton dropped points, so in a way we haven't lost anything at all really, although we dropped all three . . .'

'They've probably played better than they've ever done for a few weeks.'

'Ray Wilkins' day will come one night.'

'I'm not going to look beyond the semi-final – but I would love to lead Newcastle out at the final.'

'He never fails to hit the target. But that was a miss.'

'Maybe not goodbye, but farewell.'

'We didn't underestimate them. They were just a lot better than we thought.'

'Eighteen months ago Sweden were arguably one of the best three teams in Europe, and that would include Germany, Holland, Russia and anybody else if you like.'

And Exhibit B for the prosecution – Bobby's unique way with a tautology:

'Home advantage gives you an advantage.'

'In a year's time, he's a year older.'

'The margin is very marginal.'

'Mehmet Scholl is very two-footed.'

'Their football was exceptionally good – and they played some good football.'

Bobby's medical knowledge is second-to-none, though. Or maybe that should be zero-to-none . . .
'Nobby Solano discharged himself from hospital after the Tottenham game and he's driving, living the life and aware of who he is.'

'We can't replace Gary Speed. Where do you get an experienced player like him with a left foot and a head?'

'Gary Speed has never played better, never looked fitter, never been older.'

'They've never really allowed the Germans to have a free head.'

'Everton will want to sedate Wayne Rooney and keep the boy calm, and that is the right thing to do.'

'If you count your chickens before they've hatched, they won't lay an egg.'

'Alan Shearer has done very well for us, considering his age. We have introduced some movement into his game because he has got two good legs now. Last season he played with one leg.'

'He has four lungs and two hearts – no doubt about it.'

Bobby doesn't let his professional life interfere with his domestic life. If anything, it's the other way around:
'Newcastle have always had a poor pitch in winter. We

'don't have the better weather. My lawn up here isn't as good as my lawn in Ipswich.'

'I've just lost my house. I don't know where I'm going to sleep tonight.'

'Football's like a big marketplace, and people go to the market every day to buy their vegetables.'

'People want success. It's like coffee, they want instant.'

It's the man's sheer tactical nous that got him where he is today:
'No team won anything without a dodgy keeper.'

'The first 90 minutes of a football match are the most important.'

'Well, we got nine and you can't score more than that.'

'Anything from 1–0 to 2–0 would be a nice result.'

'We haven't had a strategic free kick all night. No one's knocked over attackers ad lib.'

'I do want to play the short ball and I do want to play the long ball. I think long and short balls is what football is all about.'

'He's very fast and if he gets a yard ahead of himself nobody will catch him.'

But at the end of the day, what makes us love Uncle Bobby is his sheer Bobbyness. Nobody else in the world of football could produce Grade A guff of this sort:
'We are all in the same bucket.'

'I've had to come out of the dressing-room because I don't want to get too excited.'

'We've dropped two points against Ipswich and I mean that sincerely.'

'Some of the goals were good, some of the goals were sceptical.'

'I'd say he's the best in Europe, if you put me on the fence.'

'We're flying on Concorde. That'll shorten the distance. That's self-explanatory.'

THE QUEEN'S ENGLISH AWARD

10. 'They haven't made many sautées forward.'
    Clive Allen
9. 'All the cul-de-sacs are closed for Scotland.'
   Joe Jordan
8. 'There is great harmonium in the dressing-room.'
   Sir Alf Ramsey
7. 'He's not going to adhere himself to the fans.'
   Alan Mullery
6. 'Well, I've seen some tackles, Jonathan, but that was the ultimatum.'
   Alan Mullery
5. 'You were a hinchpin in midfield.'
   Phil Neal
4. 'When he makes a decision, there's no arms thrown into the air and no gestating.'
   Niall Quinn
3. 'Liverpool will be without Kvarme tonight – he's illegible.'
   Jimmy Armfield
2. 'Our first goal was pure textile.'
   John Lambie
1. 'Who should be there at the far post but yours truly, Alan Shearer.'
   Colin Hendry

BEST COMMENTATOR AWARD

'Some people are on the pitch! They think it's all over . . . it is now!'

'Thomas, bursting through the midfield! It's up for grabs now . . .'

'Lord Nelson! Lord Beaverbrook! Sir Winston Churchill! Sir Anthony Eden! Clement Attlee! Henry Cooper! Lady Diana! Maggie Thatcher! Can you hear me, Maggie Thatcher? Your boys took one hell of a beating! Your boys took one hell of a beating!'

The great – and not so great – sporting occasions would be nothing without the accompanying great commentating moments. In many cases, the man in the gantry is more synonymous with a landmark event than some of the protagonists. Most people recall Kenneth Wolstenholme's contribution to 1966 at least as readily as George Cohen's. Likewise, Brian Moore's quote about Michael Thomas scoring the last-minute winner for Arsenal against Liverpool in 1989 to clinch the Championship in the last game of the season is surely more memorable than, say, Kevin Richardson. And while you mightn't remember the name of the Norwegian commentator – Bjørge Lillelien – who was beside himself at England's demise in 1981, he's made a hell of a greater impact on popular culture than Roger Albertsen or Hallvar Thoresen, the pair that actually knocked in the goals on that grim day in Oslo.

The original commentators called the players' names and politely (old boy) announced when a jolly good goal had been scored. Nowadays, the likes of Motty, Tyldesley and Tyler have all developed their own little stage acts. These guys are part comedian, part marketing exec and part interpretative artist. Make no mistake, the commentator is a playa!

All very well. But we're not interested in commentators' memorable moments. Much more entertaining are the rather more plentiful moments that the commentators wish we'd forget right away. Ninety minutes of live television with no script and only the likes of Big Ron to keep you on track is a recipe for gaffes. And it's the guff merchants rather than the cultural icons who joust for our award.

Just call us playa haters.

THE ALSO-RANS

☆Peter Drury
In a nutshell: First reserve to Clive at ITV.
Gaffta Panel Verdict: Worthy of a Gaffta Award in years to come, we feel. Keep up the good work.

'Gudjohnsen's pass allowed him to take Chelsea from behind and into the dominant position.'

'I wouldn't have the linesman's job for a big chocolate cake.'

'Smith is walking on such thin ice now that it's water.'

☆Gary Bloom
In a nutshell: Channels 4 and 5 Euro football man. Also gets all the Harchester United games on *Dream Team*.
Gaffta Panel Verdict: Versatile guffster. Perhaps needs to make one position his own.

'Zdravkov to Borimirov . . . Petrov . . . on to Hristov . . . tries to flick it off . . . doesn't really come off . . .'

'The expression of pain on his face suggests he's wearing an acid jersey.'

'To quote James Joyce: to make a mistake for one goal is unfortunate, two is foolish.'

'If that had crossed the line it would have been a goal.'

☆Jon Champion
In a nutshell: Sol Campbell of commentary. Successfully crossed BBC–ITV divide.
Gaffta Panel Verdict: Sounds like Clive. Gaffes like Clive.

'It's a general rule in international football that you try not to give too many set-pieces to Sweden.'

'There's 30 minutes gone, and we're in the first quarter of the game.'

'They seem to be in total, if not complete, control.'

☆Rob Hawthorne

In a nutshell: Upcoming Sky guffster.
Gaffta Panel Verdict: Needs to oust Parry entirely to fully showcase guff potential.

'All of West Ham's away victories have come on opponents' territory this season.'

'He runs a very tightly knit ship.'

'No score in the other game between top club and bottom club, Switzerland and Georgia.'

☆Steve Wilson

In a nutshell: Third fiddle to Motty and Davies.
Gaffta Panel Verdict: Needs to work on standing out from the guff crowd.

'There's always one upset, and the egg at the moment is heading squarely for Charlton's door.'

'The last time Italy lost in Milan, Trapattoni wasn't born. Mind you, not many people were in 1929.'

'Wome could hit this free kick with his left leg, Geremi could hit it with his right leg and Lauren could hit it dead centre.'

☆John Helm

In a nutshell: 'Who?' you say.
Gaffta Panel Verdict: That's the problem, innit?

'Such a positive move by Uruguay – bringing two players off and putting two players on.'

'West Germany's Briegel hasn't been able to get past anyone yet – that's his trademark.'

'Viv Anderson has pissed a fatness test.'

☆Ian Darke
In a nutshell: Long-time Sky man who swapped Premiership for boxing.
Gaffta Panel Verdict: Clearly punch-drunk.

'Never go for a 50–50 ball unless you're 80–20 sure of winning it.'

'And with just four minutes gone, the score is already 0–0.'

'Silvestre has had the whites of the goal in his eyes.'

☆Gerald Sinstadt
In a nutshell: Voice of the *Match of the Day* goals round-up.
Gaffta Panel Verdict: Could be Barry Davies' dad.

'If ever the Greeks needed a Trojan horse, it is now.'

'The long goalkick . . . and now, this could fall.'

'From that moment the pendulum went into reverse.'

THE NOMINEES

☆Barry Davies
In a nutshell: A fading legend tragically at ease with himself.
Gaffta Panel Verdict: Needs to buck up or it's the glue factory for this one.

Sometimes guff is more than about just the gaffes and faux pas. Sometimes it's a state of mind.

Barry Davies is proof positive that it's not just great players who eventually lose their touch. These days he's the sanctimonious old headmaster of BBC commentary, and it's easy to forget that in his heyday Davies raised more goose pimples than anyone else in the gantry.

He – far more than those lightweights Lydon, Mercury and Bowie – provided Britain's soundtrack to the '70s. With an 'Oh, I say' and a 'Goodness me' here, a 'LORIMER!' there, Bazza usually struck the right chord. It was a Franny Lee screamer for Derby against Man City that inspired one of his greatest hits – a free-wheeling, squealing, voice-cracking, climactic prog-commentary affair that serves as a sharp contrast to his tired 'Shearer, 1–0' dirges of recent years:

'This could be interesting . . . VERY INTERESTING! Look at his face! Just look at his face!'

His rivalry with Motty for the big gigs was matched only by the Clemence–Shilton stand-off of Ron Greenwood's England. While Motty had the sheepskin, the stats and the common touch, Davies always liked to preach. Even in the glory days, the potential for pontification was there. But at least back then he chose his causes well. Just such an occasion was an offside Jeff Astle goal that cost Leeds the championship and brought Don Revie roaring onto the pitch with, bizarrely, a blanket over his arm:

'Leeds will go mad! And they have every right to go mad!'

Davies was still getting it right most of the time in the '80s, realising in '86, for example, that it was an expression of low-key wonder rather than boyish excitement that was needed when Diego scored the greatest ever goal:

'Maradona . . . oooh, wonderful skill, he has Burruchaga to his left and Valdano to his left, he doesn't need them, he doesn't need any of them . . . Ohhh, you have to say that's magnificent.'

Much like Castro's little buddy himself, it was largely downhill thereafter for Davies. His flirtations with lawn tennis, ice-dancing and the Boat Race had always been suspect. And gradually, Bazza's commentaries became a miserable cocktail of look-at-me posturing over every foreign pronunciation (Ole Gunnar Sol-shire-a), pompous hectoring of cheats and miscreants, and gentleman-at-leisure disinterest in the trivial ball game he has to endure. His new partnership with Mark Lawrenson requires Davies only to punctuate Lawro's useless gags by moaning incessantly about the standard of play ('Awful, just awful'), the negativity ('The Italians have only themselves to blame, because they will not learn') and usually the standard of officiating ('I just cannot believe the French referee. Extraordinary.').

Guff for Davies, then, is more a lifestyle choice than a verbal affliction. In many ways, it is now just the occasional gaffe that makes Davies tolerable at all.

For instance, his increased ambivalence to events on the pitch has seen him seek solace in outlandish puns:

'During the Senegal game, I wonder if the French coach thought the spelling of his name had changed. They certainly had *le mare*.'

'Nicky Butt, he's another aptly named player. He joins things, brings one sentence to an end and starts another.'

For a man clearly taken with his own intellect, his grasp of fundamental physics leaves something to be desired:

'Was the ball entirely over the line? It didn't cross the line when it landed, unless it was over the line when it hit the bar.'

Trifles such as the scoreline are of minimal importance:

'It's Brazil 2, Scotland 1, so Scotland are back where they were at the start of the match.'

Mind you, when he's in the mood, Davies can do Carry-On Commentating with the best of them:

'McCarthy gave Ian Harte a special cuddle after he pulled him off.'

Nor is he slow to acknowledge impressive achievement in that department:

'They've maintained their unbeaten record between the legs.'

A good referee needs eyes in the back of his head. A good commentator's eyes might just be in the back of his head:

'The crowd thinks that Todd handled the ball – they must have seen something that nobody else did.'

Unsurprisingly for a tennis-and-boating man, Barry might not be au fait with the workings of rudimentary football equipment:

'It slid away from his left boot, which was poised with the trigger cocked.'

But, in his scholarly way, Barry has diligently committed even the game's more complex laws to memory:

'The substitutes are all on the bench, and that's where they'll start the match.'

We suggested guff was a state of mind, and Barry's cranky outlook has occasionally produced a cutting line in double-edged guff:

'Poland 0, England 0, though England are now looking the better value for their 0.'

And the magnificent . . .

'Jim Leighton is looking as sharp as a tank.'

From '70s style icon to football's answer to Simon Cowell. How the mighty have fallen.

☆Archie McPherson

In a nutshell: Scots mic-man who never quite made good.

Gaffta Panel Verdict: No shortage of guff, but hamstrung by lack of quality live fixtures.

It's an age-old tale: an optimistic young scamp believes the grass to be greener on the other side – no, we don't mean ITV – and heads off to make his fortune. But it turns out that it's not the grass that's green, and our hero returns with tail planted firmly between legs. Scots mic-man Archie McPherson would be excused a blush, because for him such a tale must be painfully close to the bone.

Dominant in football commentary north of the border, McPherson grew frustrated at Auntie's refusal to let him commentate on anyone other than Scotland. Unable to oust Motson and Davies from the really big fixtures (the two Englishmen would even usurp him from the big Scotland internationals), Archie dumped his standard-issue Beeb sheepskin★ and headed for Eurosport. A mass audience awaited his patented 'Wooaafff!' exclamation and annoying (albeit grammatically accurate) penchant for labelling international footballers 'internationalists'.

But as the bard once put it, 'all that glistens is not gold'. The mics at Eurosport Towers were not gilded after all. Archie was allowed to commentate on big fixtures all right – problem was, they were often five to ten years old! Who can forget Archie commentating on the 1992 Cup final between Manchester United and Crystal Palace – as live in 1998! How Archie's dreams must have been shattered. Motson and Davies must have been sniggering behind his back. Heartbroken, Archie took his eye off the ball, and the whole façade collapsed when Ian Wright was brought on to save the day:

'And on comes Ian Wright, who goes on to have a wonderful career at Highbury.'

Being a two-bit voiceover merchant on vintage matches (and Austrian and Belgian highlights packages) was more than Archie could bear. He returned to Scotland a broken man – the Scotty Motty, the Scotsman Motson, no longer a big player in the game.

Here's some McPherson classics, not confined to football alone:

'. . . and then there was Johan Cruyff, who at 35 has added a whole new meaning to the word Anno Domini.'

'I predicted in August that Celtic would reach the final. On the eve of that final I stand by that prediction.'

'Rangers are definitely on the back heel now.'

'And he's missed . . . and some people gathered around my television screen here are jumping up and down in an infanticide way.'

'Gillespie is playing with such eloquence.'

'Queens Park against Forfar – you can't get more romantic than that!'

*Archie McPherson's sheepskin coat is on view at the Scottish Football Museum at Hampden Park between 10 a.m. and 5 p.m. Monday to Saturday and from 11 a.m. to 5 p.m. on Sundays. Yes . . . really.

☆Tony Gubba

In a nutshell: Versatile jack-of-all-sports-commentaries.
Gaffta Panel Verdict: Mid-table Premiership status at the moment.

A tremendous long-time servant to the noble art of commentary, although to simply pigeonhole Tony as a football commentator is to deny his selflessness in the face of the needs of the BBC Sports Department over the years. For Gubba has wielded the mic for cycling, skiing, hockey, ice-dancing, table tennis, squash and bobsleigh in his time. Some even recall an impressively knowledgeable stint in a wheelchair-tennis gantry.

In the same way as play-anywhere footballers (we'd cite Phil Neville, only we mean footballers) sometimes never establish themselves in any one position, perhaps it is Gubba's very versatility that has prevented him carving a more substantial reputation as a guff merchant. He hasn't really developed a signature guff style, yet he's certainly got a gaffe or two in his locker. Here are some of the highlights from the Gubba Guffbank:

'The ageless Teddy Sheringham, at 37 now.'
What Tony gives with one hand . . .

'If Aston Villa do get a point from this it will improve their points total, of course.'
Quite a man for statistics apparently.

'Arsenal are quick to credit Bergkamp with laying on 75 per cent of their nine goals.'
Well, maybe not.

'Wigan Athletic are certain to be promoted barring a mathematical tragedy.'
Perhaps that's something you could provide, Tony.

'The ball must be as slippery as a wet baby.'
We trust Mrs Gubba looks after domestic issues.

'These two clubs had a monopoly of the domestic honours last season.'
It's not widely known that Tony keeps a two-man unicycle for parties and family gatherings.

'He was in the right place at the right time, but he might have been elsewhere on a different afternoon.'

Tony's philosophical musings give the lie to Graham Taylor's theory that time and space are the same thing.

'So often the pendulum continues to swing with the side that has just pulled themselves out of the hole.'

They ought to take care it doesn't strike them on the head as they clamber out.

'The scoreline didn't really reflect the outcome.'

Dark hints at a betting scandal among Premiership scoreboard operators?

However, if Gubba is to be remembered for any single act of guff, surely it will be his late '70s take on the first million-pound players – in particular, Trevor Francis's promotion to that exclusive club:

'Others suspect that, like the Mad Hatter at Alice's tea party with ten shillings and sixpence stuck in his hat, Trevor Francis has been condemned to complete his career under the questioning shadow of that emotive seven-figure sum.'

Less table tennis and more football, and he could have been a contender.

☆Martin Tyler

In a nutshell: Slick Sky talker may be too professional for his own good.

Gaffta Panel Verdict: Needs to loosen up a bit to really shine.

Something of a guff-watcher's nightmare, Tyler at the mic is like Steve Davis at his peak. He's always on cue, doesn't miss much, but rarely has you out of your seat and sometimes simply bores you into submission.

That said, there are several notable chinks in the Tyler armour. For one, he's become – alongside Gray and Keys –

very much a key member of the holy trinity of hype that has created the monster that is today's Premiership. And the theory that God – with a little help from Sky – invented football around about August 1992 has occasionally led Martin into trouble:

'Alan Shearer is now the most prolific Premiership goalscorer of all time.'

Martin also seems to have spent a term or two at the Barry Davies Pun Institute, and never passes up the most obvious opportunity to put his training into practice. With predictably irritating results:

'It's Ono for Japan, and it's "Oh no" for England.'

'It's ebb and flo. But Chelsea have sold Flo. Don't know what's happened to Ebb.'

And before a clash between managers Hoddle and Roeder at White Hart Lane:

'Who will be the Monarch of the Glenns today?'

Allegedly a keen pianist, Tyler extends his pun fetish to make a song and dance of any opportunity to integrate musical references into his commentary:

'His parents must have been Beatles fans, George McCartney.'

'Kewell and his gang have really hit the high notes for Australia.'

Of course anyone who has set foot in a gantry has had their 'Ooh, er missus' incidents, but occasionally Tyler rather seems to go out of his way to create those special Finbarr Saunders moments:

'Giggs drops deep into that Sheringham position where he can turn and ride defenders.'

'There was some European punishment on Thursday for Sir Alex to take on the chin, but maybe domestic pleasure is close at hand.'

And noting that Sean Bartlett had enjoyed the now-customary pre-match build-up for a Premiership player:
'He had a good romp in a reserve game in midweek and was always going to be involved today.'

No wonder he sometimes prefaces his commentary with a warning for more sensitive viewers:
'This is not a game for the puritans.'

Occasionally Tyler gets a little restless in the commentary box, fancying he could do just as decent a job as the young bucks on the pitch:
'If you're old enough, you're good enough.'

Harsh reality usually sinks in eventually:
'The ageless Dennis Wise, now in his 30s . . .'

For all his smoothness, one peculiarity of Tyler's commentary is his weakness for rather, shall we say, oxymoronical sentences:
'He had an eternity to play that ball, but he took too long over it.'

'McCarthy shakes his head in agreement with the referee.'

'Ian Baird is dashing around like a steamroller up front.'
Make up your mind, man.

☆Alan Parry

In a nutshell: Precariously positioned on the Sky commentating periphery.
Gaffta Panel Verdict: Numbers are his guff Achilles heel.

A dyed-in-the-sheepskin Liverpool fan, Parry plugs away on the periphery of the commentating game, having been gradually edged down the Sky rankings by young guns like Rob Hawthorne. He seems to have formed an unholy alliance with Brian Marwood, which seems peculiar considering the pair's almost polar-opposite opinions of Arsenal. While Parry makes his distaste clear in every broadcast (even if Arsenal aren't playing), ex-Gunner Marwood regularly thrills to every shrug of Henry and co.'s shoulders.

The two are rather more compatible when it comes to guff, between them presenting Sky pay-per-view victims with an almost entirely sense-free experience for their fivers.

Here are some choice cuts from the Parry guffbank:

'The first major trophy of the afternoon will be decided later.'
Parry puts the Carling Cup in its place.

'Cleland was the victim of his own downfall.'
Landed badly?

'Villa will probably play a lot worse than this and lose.'
They surely will.

'That's referee Mike Reed's 50th booking of the season, which works out at an average of six a game.'
Don't forget to carry the two, Alan . . .

'Ritchie has now scored 11 goals, exactly double the number he scored last season.'
. . . or indeed the one.

'Liverpool are currently halfway through an unbeaten 12-match run.'
That's better.

'The Liverpool players are passing the cup down the line like a newborn baby. Although when they are back in the dressing-room they will probably fill it with champagne, something you should never do to a baby.'
Unlike Tony Gubba, Parry is the responsible one in his household.

'He will probably wake up after having sleepless nights thinking about that one.'
Not the baby, hopefully.

'The shot from Laws was precise but wide.'
About as precise as the commentary.

'Lampard, as usual, arrived in the nick of time, but it wasn't quite soon enough.'
Might as well have taken his time.

'The ball was literally glued to the back of his foot – into the back of the net.'
That's one packet of glue we'd take back to the shop.

'He had no chance of beating Schmeichel from there, but it was always worth a try.'
Raising a glass to the art of futility.

☆ Clive Tyldesley

In a nutshell: Big Ron's straight man before the shame.
Gaffta Panel Verdict: Remains to be seen if he can cut it as a solo artist.

For many years Clive was the Andrew Ridgeley of football commentary's standard-bearing duo. However, Big Ron's fall from grace has relegated him back into the pack of virtually indistinguishable ITV commentators also populated by Peter Drury and Jon Champion.

Of course, Clive will always retain one distinguishing characteristic – he is a rabid Manchester United fan and will make no attempt to conceal that fact during a broadcast.

In an unofficial survey of TV repair shops (which excluded the greater Manchester area, large sections of Surrey and all of Asia), it was found that 94 per cent of all screen breakages are reported the day after a televised Man United Champions League tie. In all cases, thorough cross-referencing identified Clive as the commentator.

To be honest, this kind of thing can grate after a while:
'Roy Keane is such a driving force! He's a powerful man. I'll tell you, there's been a few times after questions when I've been reduced to stutters by a stare from Roy. He's a strong man on and off the pitch!'

Especially when it gets even more . . . well . . . revealing:
'Those trophy-lifting fingers of Roy Keane's are getting itchy. Hard man – hard to satisfy, hard to beat.'

Sometimes, Clive's raging bias can manifest itself a little more subtly. Cast your minds back to United's ill-fated Big Cup semi-final with Bayer Leverkusen a few years back. First Bayer star, Ze Roberto, picked up his third booking of the tournament for an innocuous enough challenge:
'He'll miss the next game, which could be the final.'

Then Nicky Butt did likewise. Cue despair:
'He will miss the final.'

Magnificently, Clive stayed loyal to United misfit Diego Forlan even after his barren start at Old Trafford. In fact, Clive preferred to look at it this way:
'Forlan has played in 15 games now . . . and he's nearly scored in all of them.'

Of course, Clive's United devotion paid off big style in 1999, on that 'balmy night in Barcelona', which he has since referred to at least twice in every commentary. Then Clive's commentary was single-handedly responsible for United's grand added-time larceny:

'What's this? Ninety minutes on the clock and Manchester United haven't scored. They have to score, they always score . . . Sheringhaaaaammmmm!'

The downside, unfortunately, is that he's tried the same thing ever since. The aforementioned Leverkusen disaster brought similar vain appeals to the gods:

'They need to score. United always score.'

Big Ron – a not-entirely neutral arbitrator himself – did nothing to rid Clive of the habit, even shamelessly encouraging him to save the day during another United exit to Porto:

'Go on. Put one of your signs on it quick.'

Sadly for United, Clive's less-than-convincing response couldn't produce another flukey injury-time toe-poke:

'Ahh . . . they don't always score but, boy, do they need one now.'

What's the betting we don't hear about this one for the next hundred years?

The United factor aside, Clive's double act with Ron brought much-needed light relief to the less glamorous Euro nights. Usually, Clive played Little to Ron's Large:

Clive: So, Ron, who do you fancy?
Ron: Not you, Clive, that's for sure!

Ron: Tell you what, Clive, Cole has missed a stick-on there, I would have put my mortgage on him in that situation.
Clive: Tell me, Ron, how much is your mortgage?
Ron: I haven't got one, Clive.

After Zola took a kick in the wotsits and rolled around clutching them in agony:

Clive: Hmmm, I'm not sure where exactly he was injured there.

Ron: Just inside his own half I think, Clive.

Mind you, Ron was never quite so willing to go to canvas when Clive brought a punchline of his own into the ring:

Clive: Earlier in the season a substitution was delayed because the player had to remove rings and chains. That didn't happen much in your day, Ron?

Ron: Not the chains.

Clive: It'd take half the night to get your chains off, Ron.

Ron: [Silence]

Of course, Clive was there on the night Ron went overboard, and now it is he who must prove that he can stay afloat without his big orange life jacket. The signs aren't good. Makeshift partnerships with the dozy Uncle Bobby or the jack-the-lad Andy Townsend just haven't clicked so far. Still, if Clive can find the right foil, he has a strong enough guff track record to soon get back among the main players.

Here are some of his personal career highlights:

'He is the man who has been brought on to replace Pavel Nedved. The irreplaceable Pavel Nedved.'

'He's not George Best, but, then again, no one is.'

'He went through a non-existent gap.'

'One or two of their players aren't getting any younger.'

'If they come back, it's a night we'll remember for a long time. But that's a capital if.'

'David O'Leary's poker face betrays the emotions.'

Clive has also expressed some reservations about the NHS that will concern Tony Blair:

'Gary Neville is in hospital, where Manchester United fear he may have broken his foot.'

And he regularly donates the contents of his wardrobe to strikers who have recovered their form:

'Quite literally, you would not have put your shirt on him.'

Credit where it's due, though: when it comes to reading the shape of a game, Clive has few equals:

'This is the half of the field where Bayer do most of their damage.'

That is a spotter's badge.

☆ Brian Moore

In a nutshell: Grand old uncle of footie coverage.

Gaffta Panel Verdict: Along with David Coleman, brought the guff tablets down from Mt Sinai.

Good old Mooro, God rest his soul. Where would English football have been in the 1970s and 1980s without him? He was still around in the 1990s, of course, but, like Jimmy Hill, by that time the increasingly crowded world of football coverage had nearly edged him out. Whether presenting *The Big Match* (desk replete with office equipment, including the huge telephone he never used) or commentating on a big match, Mooro's avuncular, slightly befuddled demeanour somehow provided reassurance that we were partaking in a small way in a great tradition: the continuous tapestry of football as it spanned the decades. We shall not see his like again. We probably won't hear his like again either, because Mooro had a singular style of commentary impossible to reproduce or emulate.

His swansong was that infamous moment in World Cup 1998, as David Batty stepped up to take the penalty kick that would send England crashing out of the tournament, defeated again by ancient adversary Argentina.

Mooro: [to co-commentator Kevin Keegan] Quickly, Kevin – will he score?
Keegan: Yes.
The correct answer, Kevin, was 'no'.

Mooro's unique style can be broken down into a few broad headings, basically organised along the lines of things the great man had some measure of difficulty with, at least in the heat of the commentary moment.

STATISTICS:
'Rosenborg have won 66 games, and they've scored in all of them.'
Rock-solid logic there.

'Newcastle, of course, unbeaten in their last five wins.'
The same logic again, its irrefutability doubly demonstrated.

'The familiar sight of Liverpool lifting the League Cup for the first time.'
This is not so rock solid.

'That's the 34th time he's played for his country here tonight.'
There's nonsense, damned nonsense and statistics.

'Manchester United have never beaten an Italian side on two legs in European competition.'
They have managed to beat all their one-legged opponents, though.

'Sitting on the Watford bench is Ernie Whalley's brother, Tom. Both Welshmen.'
What are the odds?

'One hundred and twenty thousand Barcelona fans go to their home games, and they're all here tonight.'
Mooro's way of saying there's a capacity crowd.

METAPHORS:
'Zidane has the body of a bear, the mind of a fox and . . . ah . . . terrific skills . . .'
Mooro paints himself into a metaphorical corner.

'He has the brain of a refrigerator.'
No need to be insulting.

'It's just a sea of voices here at the moment.'
Mooro's all at sea with this maritime metaphor.

'Everybody thought the Saudis were coming here as chopping blocks.'
Unlikely that the Saudis thought that, or they'd never have got on the plane.

'He's a schizophrenic of a keeper.'
Tastefully done, Mooro.

'Pearce with the kick, the last throw for England.'
And possibly the final straw for the listening public.

'When you speak to Barry Fry, it's like completing a 1,000-piece jigsaw.'
Mooro found similes equally troublesome.

BIOLOGY:

'Souness's football brain was working at a hundred miles an hour there!'
At that rate, it's surprising that Souness could manage to stay within the confines of the stadium.

'Mark Ward has only got size-five boots, but he sure packs a hell of a punch with them.'
That's not Queensberry Rules.

'You can see how O'Leary is absolutely racked with pain, and realises it.'
If only he hadn't realised it, there would have been no need for painkillers.

'The news from Guadalajara, where the temperature is 96 degrees, is that Falcao is warming up.'
You heard it first from Mooro.

AND THE REST . . .

'Adams is stretching himself, looking for Seaman.'
'Ooh, Matron', etc. . . .

'There are those who've had his critics.'
'Ooh, Matron', part II.

'Mark Hughes – Sparky by name, sparky by nature. The same can be said of Brian McClair.'
That must cause some confusion on the field.

'I wonder if Manchester United are missing the absence of Bruce.'
Surely Bruce wasn't playing that badly?

'They've flown in from all over the world, the Rest of the World team.'

Mooro gave it the full gun with pre-match research.

'History is all about todays and not yesterdays.'
Dictionary for Mr Moore . . .

'This is going to be a very long 30 minutes with 26 minutes left.'
Those post-match four minutes might be quite boring, all right.

'Bryan Robson wears his shirt on his sleeve.'
Must be a problem for throw-ins.

'The whole team stopped as one man, but Arkwright in particular.'
So Arkwright stopped, then?

'And now that we have the formalities over, we'll have the national anthems.'
At last the real action starts.

'Wayne Clarke, one of the famous Clarke family, and he's one of them, of course.'
Can't argue with that.

And finally, what is arguably the definitive Mooro comment:
'The Champions League winners stand to make £10 million in prize money. That's before any money they can make on programme sales, hot dogs and the like.'

WINNER

☆ John Motson

In a nutshell: Vaguely troubling flagship Beeb gantryman.

Gaffta Panel Verdict: Devotion to the cause, years of service and occasional moments of strangeness mean that Motty is up there in a league of his own.

No one could accuse John Motson of lack of commitment to the game. The man lives, breathes and most likely eats football. Renowned for commentating on Subbuteo matches at home to warm up for big games, he brings a singular devotion to his job. Whilst he could – and does – talk for England, he cuts a disconcertingly taciturn figure in the *Football Focus* studio whenever Stubbsy drags him in for a spot of extracurricular punditry duty. It seems that Motty is far less comfortable being a talking head than merely a speaking voice. As anyone with a high-definition widescreen television will tell you, perhaps that's for the best.

It's hard to pin down exactly what makes Motty the man that he is. In an attempt to get to the bottom of this mystery, we've categorised some of his top quotes along the lines of things that give him trouble.

COLOUR TROUBLE:

'Northern Ireland were in white, which was quite appropriate because three inches of snow had to be cleared from the pitch before kick-off.'

Camouflage gear is often the difference between victory and defeat in a football match.

'The referee is wearing the same yellow-coloured top as the Slovakian goalkeeper. I'd have thought the UEFA official would have spotted that, but perhaps he's been deafened by the noise of this crowd.'

The UEFA official is presumably either a bat or a whale.

'Nearly all the Brazilian supporters are wearing yellow shirts – it's a fabulous kaleidoscope of colour!'

Motty's kaleidoscope must be on the blink.

'It must be like being stuck in the middle of a giant Outspan.'

In fact, Motty, sitting amongst Dutch fans is not much like being stuck inside an orange.

'For those of you watching in black and white, Spurs are in the yellow strip.'

The all-time Motty colours classic.

NUMBER TROUBLE:

'If David Beckham claims that goal, it will be only the second goal he has scored for England . . . well, no, it won't be . . . it'll be the fourth or fifth free kick, I think . . . but certainly the one in Sapporo is the one we remember most in recent times . . . but how often has he changed the direction of the game for England?'

How often has Motty changed the direction of this sentence?

'You couldn't count the number of moves Alan Ball made . . . I counted four, and possibly five.'

Other people can also count to five, Motty . . .

'I've just heard that in the other match Real Madrid have just scored. That makes the score, if my calculations are correct, 4–3! But I'm only guessing!'

. . . in fact, we doubt that you can count to five yourself . . .

'I've lost count of how many chances Helsingborg have had. It's at least five.'

. . . you've proved us wrong . . .

'In a sense it's a one-man show . . . except that there are two men involved, Hartson and Berkovic, and a third man, the goalkeeper.'
. . . but unfortunately you can count to three.

'He's not quite at 110 per cent fitness.'
At least 10 per cent off.

'It's Arsenal 0, Everton 1, and the longer it stays like that, the more you've got to fancy Everton to win.'
Intensive statistical analysis shows Motty to be correct.

'There is still nothing on the proverbial scoreboard.'
The actual scoreboard might have said something else.

'And how ironic that the time on the clock is 66.'
Ah yes, Motty. England score against Germany in the 66th minute, and they also beat Germany to the World Cup in 1966. How apt. Now, you won't go labouring the point, will you? Oh, you will . . .

'And what a time to score! Twenty-two minutes gone!'
What a time. All you have to do to make it sixty-six is multiply it by three.

'And is that the moment when Sven-Göran Eriksson stopped being a lucky manager?'
The moment? Pick any minute corresponding to a year in which Germany beat England.

FOREIGN PLACES TROUBLE:
'England are playing this game in Bratislava because there's a much better atmosphere than in Prague!'
That, and maybe also because Prague is the capital of the Czech Republic, not Slovakia.

'The World Cup is a truly international event.'
A few countries other than England have got involved over the years.

'And that's England's finest victory over the Germans since the war!'
Say no more, Motty. We know what you mean.

'Middlesbrough are withdrawing Maccarone the Italian, Nemeth the Slovakian and Stockdale the right back.'
Motty invents a new nationality.

BREAKFAST OBSESSION:
During World Cup 2002, Motty became rather fixated on the fact that while the matches were being played in the evening in Japan and Korea, it was actually early in the day in the UK.

'Just one minute of overtime, so you can put the eggs on now if you like.'
Useful cookery information from Motty.

'You can have your breakfast with Batistuta and your cornflakes with Crespo.'
Yes, yes . . . and your orange juice with Owen and your fry with Figo, etc., etc.

'I can confirm that Trevor Brooking did have his own eggs and bacon before setting off this morning.'
A nation waited with bated breath for confirmation.

'England will be having Sweden for breakfast.'
Not really, as it turned out.

'Hold on to your cups and glasses . . . you can smash them now, David Beckham has scored!'
Motty provides instructions to the audience at home as England go one up against the Argies.

WORKING PRACTICES TROUBLE:

'Trevor Brooking's notes are getting wet with the rain. I must lend him some of the perspex I always bring to cover mine.'

A disturbing window into Motty's soul.

'It's so exciting we're talking at the same time for the first time ever!'

An unforgivable lapse. Surprised he and Trevor Brooking weren't both sacked.

'I was about to say, before something far more interesting interrupted . . .'

You can't stay on top of your game unless you're your own worst critic.

'INTERESTING' FACTS TROUBLE:

'Actually, none of the players are wearing earrings. Kjeldberg, with his contact lenses, is the closest we can get.'

Well, earrings and contact lenses are essentially the same thing . . .

'It's so different from the scenes in 1872, at the Cup final none of us can remember.'

Ah, yes, we remember it well.

'Paul Gascoigne has recently become a father and been booked for over-celebrating.'

Best to limit those celebrations to friends and family.

'The atmosphere here is literally electric.'

Thunderstorm? Static electricity problem? Who knows?

'It's a football stadium in the truest sense of the word.'

In the truest sense of the word . . . what?

'And I suppose Spurs are nearer to being out of the FA Cup now than at any other time since the first half of this season, when they weren't ever in it anyway.'

They were a good way from being out of it then, really.

'Chelsea haven't got any out-and-out strikers on the bench unless you count Zenden, who's more of a winger.'

We won't count him then.

PRAISE TROUBLE:

'There's been no conviction about England . . . BUT THERE'S PLENTY OF CONVICTION NOW AS WAYNE ROONEY . . .'

Motty's commentary can turn on a sixpence.

'Oh, that's good running on the run.'

Running on the run is even quicker than ordinary running.

'And Seaman, just like a falling oak, manages to change direction.'

Agile trees, those oaks.

'I can't fault Mark Palios too highly.'

High praise.

'I have to say, he's done as well as anyone out there.'

Not at all patronising, Motty is impressed with Japanese player Nakata's performance for Roma against Liverpool.

MATCH ANALYSIS TROUBLE:

No football match would ever be complete without Motty's attempts to elucidate the patterns and trends on the field of play that ordinary mortals cannot perceive.

'Well, frankly, it's embarrassing.'

Motty's verdict after a sustained spell of Macedonian pressure against England.

'England have dug themselves out of some deep holes in recent times.'
You only have to dig down about 7,000 miles to reach the other side of the world.

'That shot might not have been as good as it might have been.'
Mighty strong words.

'The goals made such a difference to the way this game went.'
Normally, goals don't matter too much.

'Not the first half you might have expected, even though the score might suggest that it was.'
Those pesky goals clouding the issue again.

'The match has become quite unpredictable, but it still looks as though Arsenal will win the cup.'
Not completely unpredictable then.

'The game is balanced in Arsenal's favour.'
On balance, Motty's probably right.

'The unexpected is always likely to happen.'
Should have seen it coming.

'The match was settled at either side of half-time.'
Make up your mind, Motty.

'That's an old Ipswich move – O'Callaghan crossing for Mariner to drive over the bar.'
Sadly, probably true.

'Whether that was a penalty or not, the referee thought otherwise.'
Contrary man, that ref.

'Just look at Keegan's face, he's got a look of resignation . . . I don't mean, of course, about his managerial position, but rather about today's game.'

Don't backtrack, Motty. We know what you meant.

ANATOMY TROUBLE:

'I know that Gareth Barry has been told by Howard Wilkinson to take a long hard look at these with his left foot.'

Who says that Wilko asks the impossible of his players?

'Bruce has got the taste of Wembley in his nostrils.'

Motty remembers from his O level biology class that taste buds are not the only determinants of taste.

'OOH, MATRON' TROUBLE:

Even single-minded Motty isn't immune to the 'Ooh, Matron' curse:

'Brazil – they're so good it's like they are running around the pitch playing with themselves.'

A disturbing image, if ever there was one.

'Beattie can't generate enough power to beat Seaman from that distance.'

Guess that explains what the Saints pin-up was doing in Oleg Luzhny's pocket all day.

THE MIXED METAPHOR AWARD

10.'In the Scottish Cup you only get one crack at the cherry against Rangers or Celtic.'
   Tom Ferrie

9. 'I can see the carrot at the end of the tunnel.'
   Stuart Pearce

8. 'The run of the ball is not in our court at the moment.'
   Phil Neal

7. 'The lads have run their socks into the ground.'
   Alex Ferguson

6. 'Butcher goes forward as Ipswich throw their last trump card into the fire.'
   Byron Butler

5. 'Glenn is putting his head in the frying pan.'
   Ossie Ardiles

4. 'Our fans have been branded with the same brush.'
   Ron Atkinson

3. 'I was feeling as sick as the proverbial donkey.'
   Mick McCarthy

2. 'We could be putting the hammer in Luton's coffin.'
   Ray Wilkins

1. 'Real Madrid are like a rabbit in the glare of the headlights in the face of Manchester United's attacks. But this rabbit comes with a suit of armour in the shape of two precious away goals.'
   George Hamilton

THE **GAFFTA** AWARDS

BEST SUPPORTING COMMENTATOR AWARD

The co-commentator is a relatively recent invention. It used to be that Kenneth Wolstenholme, or whoever, would perch alone in the gantry, describing the action and perhaps proffering the odd opinion. It often made for unexciting listening, boiling down more or less to a litany of names. 'Hurst . . . to Charlton . . . back to Hurst . . .' The problem essentially was that while the commentator may have been very articulate and in possession of a good speaking voice, he usually lacked the kind of credentials that would enable him to analyse or otherwise speak authoritatively about proceedings on the pitch.

And so the co-commentator entered the match-coverage equation. Briefed to provide on-the-spot analysis and opinion during match-time, the co-commentator soon became much, much more than simply the commentator's sidekick. A boon to the PFA, this new role provided employment for otherwise unemployable ex-footballers. How Chris 'the ball just crept either side of the post' Kamara would have earned a living outside the world of football is anyone's guess (most likely by singing bluesy rock numbers in holiday resorts), but thanks to Rupert Murdoch and his multimedia empire, Kamara bestrides the high street like an affluent consumerist colossus, spending money like the comfortably middle-class broadcaster he is.

Co-commentary has some precipitous pitfalls too, of course . . . But the sorry plight of Ron Atkinson need not detain us here. Instead, look on the bright side and enjoy this very special Gaffta Awards category.

THE ALSO-RANS

☆Andy Townsend
In a nutshell: Made to look good on ITV panel by McCoist and Earle.
Gaffta Panel Verdict: Perseverance with the Tactics Truck could have made him a contender.

'I'm sure Heinz will be in Karel Bruckner's thinking mind now.'

'Dick Advocaat's furious. He's just kicked the bucket, I think!'

On Thierry Henry:
'He's like a laxative, he goes straight through you and there's nothing you can do about it.'

An intravenous boost for Michael Owen:
'Once he's got confidence in his veins, he's a real threat.'

☆Joe Royle
In a nutshell: First name on the list for yo-yo clubs. Up and down like a bride's nighty!
Gaffta Panel Verdict: Needs to do more than sun himself at major tournaments if he's ever to pick up a gong.

'They've scored four goals without our keeper having a save to make.'

'As the old-timers say, don't rub 'em, count 'em.'

'Butina hasn't been too convincing up to now. He could even be accused of chocolate wrists for young Wayne's goal.'

'Dare I say it, Heinz has given them more variety.'

☆Chris Waddle

In a nutshell: Once Hoddle's partner in musical crime, he now takes rare co-commenting opportunities to match his pal guff for guff.

Gaffta Panel Verdict: As accomplished behind the mic as from the spot. Just needs to be given his head.

'That's no remedy for success.'

'If that had gone in, I don't think Van Der Sar would have saved it.'

'The Swedish back four is amongst the tallest in the World Cup. Their average age is 7 ft 4 in.'

Stating his mathematically precise credentials for the Sheffield Wednesday job:
'We had about eight games, we won two or three, drew one and lost a couple.'

THE NOMINEES

☆ Ron Atkinson

In a nutshell: Tanned, bejewelled co-commentary colossus who plunged from grace like Buddy Holly.

Gaffta Panel Verdict: Tell you what, this lad can play a bit!

Before he tumbled to disgrace in the Stade Louis II, Big Orange Ron was known as football punditry's great linguistic innovator. We've rewarded him for being the only ex-Oxford United player to create his own language. However, while the jewel-strewn genius is rightly lauded for his pioneering phraseology, many people forget the equally phenomenal contribution Ron has made to the timeless art of guff. However, while less distinguished guff merchants are betrayed by the folly of their own nonsense, Ron's occasional faux pas only further underline his unique contribution to the game.

FOOTBALL KNOWLEDGE:

Football may be a beautiful game, but it's not a simple one. Establishing the mastery that Ron exudes takes years of experience and training. Witness these astonishing insights from the big 'gold-horse'. It just doesn't have a price . . .

'They've done the old-fashioned things well: they've kicked the ball, they've headed it . . .'

'I've had this sneaking feeling throughout the game that it's there to be won.'

'Woodcock would have scored, but his shot was too perfect.'

'They must go for it now as they have nothing to lose but the match.'

'Now Manchester United are 2–1 down on aggregate, they are in a better position than when they started the game at 1–1.'

MASTERY OF LANGUAGE:

(a) The metaphor

Co-commentating apprentices like Beglin and Waddle may think it's sufficient to arm yourself with a single metaphor before commenting on an incident. Not Ron. Real legends come to the party with metaphors and similes aplenty, and do not hesitate to lump the whole lot into a single sentence if the situation demands. Confusion? We prefer to call it genius:

'Beckenbauer has really gambled all his eggs.'

'Tony Adams – he's the rock that the team has grown from.'

'He sliced the ball when he had it on a plate.'

'Someone in the England team will have to grab the ball by the horns.'

'They've picked their heads up off the ground and they now have a lot to carry on their shoulders.'

'He's treading on dangerous water there . . .'

'Chelsea look like they've got a couple more gears left in the locker.'

(b) Clarity

Ron's spent long enough wrestling with the *Sun* crossword to know that people don't like to be kept guessing. While peppering his co-commentary with fascinating insights and useful facts, Ron's precise language skills ensure that even the non-initiated can closely follow events on the pitch:

'There's a little triangle – five left-footed players.'

'For me, the book's still open on Totti.'

'You think he'd chance his hat there.'

'Liverpool are outnumbered numerically in midfield.'

'I would also think that the replay showed it to be worse than it actually was.'

'He's not only a good player, but he's spiteful in the nicest sense of the word.'

'The keeper was unsighted – he still didn't see it.'

'You half fancied that to go in as it was rising and dipping at the same time.'

'That was Pelé's strength – holding people off with his arm.'

DECISIVENESS:

It's no picnic putting your neck on the line with bold predictions every week, you know. Look what happened to Rodney Marsh's hair and Lawro's tache, for example. Ron, in the best tradition of plucky punditry, is never afraid to call it early:

'I wouldn't say Ginola is the best left-winger in the Premiership, but there are none better.'

'Well, either side could win it, or it could be a draw.'

'City will want to win this one.'

AWARENESS:

High-profile purveyors of punditry have to look over their shoulders continually. There's always a smart arse keen to twist their words for comic effect. With that in mind, Ron's eventual demise was all the more surprising. Such an experienced campaigner has always known the value of choosing his words carefully:

'Moreno thought that the full back was gonna come up behind and give him one really hard.'

'There's lots of balls dropping off people.'

'Every time Zidane comes inside, Roberto Carlos just goes bonking down the wing.'

'He dribbles a lot and the opposition don't like it – you can see it all over their faces.'

'Zidane is not very happy, because he's suffering from the wind.'

'Stoichkov's playing on the wing; in this situation he likes to come in and scalp the centre-half.'

'I think Sir Alex might have been thinking about pulling Giggsy off . . . but that might be an incentive to stay on.'

RAW TALENT:

There aren't enough lollipops and little eyebrows in the world to match the style on show in the gantry when Ron gives it the full gun. Class will out. Spotter's badge, sir.

'I never comment on referees and I'm not going to break the habit of a lifetime for that prat.'

'A ten-foot keeper really should have stopped that.'

'They've come out at half-time and gone bang.'

'The lad throws it further than I go on holiday.'

'. . . and Schmeichel extends and grows even bigger than he is.'

'I think that was a moment of cool panic there.'

☆Andy Gray

In a nutshell: Took the Murdoch shilling many years ago and entered the airless, vaguely frightening world of Sky Sports. Is their co-commentator of choice.

Gaffta Panel Verdict: On the pitch he was classy, but high profile notwithstanding, an innate lack of finesse in the gantry means that Gray has to huff and puff a lot to make any headway. Always gives it the 110 per cent – but this doesn't always translate into guff.

In a way, Andy Gray is one of the game's true pioneers. Some point to Andy's role alongside Martin Tyler and Richard Keys in the creation of 'The Greatest League in the World' as his finest hour. Along the way to this achievement, he has pulled off some admirable feats of bluster. But this is nothing compared to the extraordinary work he has done in the research and development of the PACE (Pace, Awareness, Calibration and Evaluation) scale, a complex measurement system now used by all commentators to assess the speed of a frontman with a little bit of what Big Ron might call 'turbo' at his disposal. As far as Andy is concerned, the PACE scale operates, in reverse order of paciness, something like this:

8. **Tell you what, Martin, the little number seven has** a bit of pace.
7. **Watch the Norwegian fella. He's big, brave, and** pacy.
6. **They might do a double-banking job on the left-winger. He has got** bags of pace.
5. **Heh, heh, heh, Richard. There's no substitute for** lightning pace.
4. **If you stand off this fella, he'll kill you.** Unbelievable pace.

3. If this fella can get it out of his feet, he has got frightening pace.

2. What an out ball he gives them. This guy has got pace to burn.

1. You just can't legislate for genuine pace.

THE GRAY GUFFBANK:

'That's bread and butter straight down the goalkeeper's throat.'

'I watched the game and I saw an awful lot of it.'

'It's what I call one of those "indefensible ones" – you can't defend against them.'

'The one thing that tackle wasn't was high and dangerous.'

'For my money, Duff servicing people from the left with his balls in there is the best option.'

'People say footballers have terrible taste in music, but I would dispute that. In the car at the moment I've got The Corrs, Cher, Phil Collins, Shania Twain and Rod Stewart.'

☆Brian Marwood

In a nutshell: Sky second co-commentary fiddle happy with his lot. Possibly.

Gaffta Panel Verdict: Perma-vacillating Brian is a guffster with bags of promise.

As a player, Brian Marwood could have been the son George Graham never had: a tricky winger not afraid to put a bit of effort in. Anders Limpar certainly paid the price for following in his footsteps. Nowadays, he has turned into an all-round good egg, happy to help Gordon Taylor with whatever it is they do at the PFA and willing to do any Sky co-commentary gig Andy Gray doesn't fancy. One of Marwood's proudest co-commentating moments to date was when he garnered the first spotter's badge to be awarded outside of the ITV network. You'll learn later that the spotter's badge is Big Ron's much-sought-after prize for perceptive players with the vision to see a pass early. Unsurprisingly, it was chief Ron plagiarist Andy Gray who officiated at this ceremony. Taking time out from pressing buttons and pulling levers in the Sky *Monday Night Football* control room, Gray rather made a mockery of the time-honoured award by rewarding Marwood for simply remarking that Sheffield Wednesday were a little suspect in the air, minutes before they shipped another header from a corner.

In truth, Marwood deserved this treasured – if ill-gotten – metaphorical memento, mainly for spotting that you can still make a handsome living from the media game with a command of English that seems to be the fruits of a weekend TEFL course in Burnley.

You see, Marwood really isn't very good at talking. In UK terms, he'd probably be ranked somewhere outside the top 35 million or so talkers out there. But, rather than let such details deflect him from a career in broadcasting, he's made a virtue of necessity. Never one to stick his neck out anyway, Marwood now neatly operates on the principle that if they can't understand you, they certainly can't say you're wrong.

In his debut season as a pundit, Marwood's chief tactic in this cunning ruse was his regular use of the double negative:

'Ian Wright is missing the absence of Dennis Bergkamp.'

A subtle reference to a Highbury rift or simply another rubbish attempt at talking? Nobody really knew, and there was the genius of it. The mark of a true star, however, is the ability to adapt. And as the savvy football-watching public eventually cottoned on to his caper, Marwood magnificently patented the triple negative – an impenetrable commentary code that enabled him to back both nags in a two-horse race.

Here are three examples. Go ahead – try and make sense of any of them:

'You certainly wouldn't bet against him not converting that chance.'

'I'm not sure they won't be looking not to substitute him this early.'

'I don't think there are too many people betting against him not scoring from the spot.'

You've no idea, have you? So whether the chance goes wide, the sub comes on or the spotter is saved, Brian's got it covered. The only wonder is that Trevor Brooking didn't think of it first.

The downside of becoming reliant on this approach is that, when shorn of his confuse-and-conquer safety net, Marwood has found himself unable to commit to the simplest statement of fact.

So you'll regularly hear the likes of:

'It's his first cap, so I would say he's not got a lot of experience at this level.'

'There's still 45 minutes to go – for both sides, I would guess.'

'The ball could have gone anywhere and almost did.'

☆Chris Kamara

In a nutshell: Sky pundit/co-commentator yet to make that breakthrough to the top flight.

Gaffta Panel Verdict: Excitable Chris is a sitcom waiting to be made.

In the mid-1990s, Chris Kamara abandoned lower-league football management in favour of a new career in lower-league football punditry. There he remains to this day, having gradually insinuated himself into the fabric of Sky Sports. Whether perching uncomfortably on a couch with *Football Extra* co-host Rob McCaffrey, or roaring his head off at the McAlpine Stadium to the bemusement of Jeff Stelling in the Sky *Soccer Saturday* studio, Kamara is a blokey, vaguely comedic presence. He can take a joke (as when Barry Fry likened him to Lionel Richie) and he can deliver one (as when he described the Stadium of Light crèche as Jason McAteer's playroom). But it's for unintentional humour that Kamara is most valued.

His main problem is his sheer level of enthusiasm for football. Two or three minutes into every match he starts to get far too excited. The ultimate victim is the English language. Don't look to Chris for crystal clarity, or even logical sense, when it comes to match reports:

'It really is an amazing result! Nil–nil at half-time!'

'It [the ball] just crept either side of the post.'

'Traore was there for . . . [huge pause] . . . good measure.'

'That's fantastic there . . . whatever that is.'

'Stern John wide with the header. He's really suffering from confidence.'

'It's real end-to-end stuff, but unfortunately it's all up at Forest's end.'

'They've one man to thank for that goal, Alan Shearer. And they've also got to thank Alan Wiley, the referee.'
(This is doubly genius since Craig Bellamy was the goalscorer.)

You can tell he's an ex-manager. It's the little gems of insight that give it away:

'For Burnley to win they are going to have to score.'

'They only count when they go in the goal.'

He knows just what's going through a player's mind:

'He's thinking, "Don't look where I'm going to put it because I am going to put it where you don't think I am, and you can dive to the right and look over your left shoulder to see the ball go into the net."'

He does seem to have some difficulty using some of the English language's most common phrases:

'The atmosphere here is thick and fast.'

'Barnsley have started off the way they mean to begin.'

'Statistics are there to be broken.'

'He went down like a pack of cards.'

'It was six and half a dozen, and six won.'

'If you don't buy a ticket, you can't win the raffle! And his number is coming up now! Number one! And it's 3–2!'

And Chris can't have been listening in science class when he was a lad. He hasn't quite mastered the usage of units of measurement:

'They're leading 3–0 and Charlton fans will feel they've deserved every second of it.'

'Now they have got an extra yard of doubtness in their minds.'

But one thing Chris definitely is a master of is the double-positive statement:

'Not only has he shown Junior Lewis the red card, but he's sent him off.'

'Now both teams want the ball. Sheffield want the ball, and so do United.'

He also has the much-prized 'Ooh, Matron' factor:

'How did you straighten him out, because he credits you with that?'

Chris asks Graham Taylor how he got Elton John fancying girls again. Maybe.

And he clearly knows a little bit too much about a certain Liverpool player:

'Big player, big heart, big occasion, big everything.'

☆Mark Bright

In a nutshell: Confused former player like a bull in the co-commentary china shop.

Gaffta Panel Verdict: Could hit the big leagues with enough airtime.

Former Crystal Palace star and Ian Wright sidekick Mark Bright was once asked which current player he'd compare himself with. 'Thierry Henry, I'd like to think,' he ventured. No doubt if asked to liken himself to an orator, he'd have gone for Churchill.

In truth, Brighty's public-speaking skills are as devoid of va-va-voom as his football was in days of yore. Frequently paired with Barry Davies on the Beeb, he has eradicated what little was left of schoolmaster Bazza's hair with his unrelenting persecution of the Queen's English:

'The crowd will be looking for Vieri to inspirate them.'

'The marking was non-extinct there.'

'He's got all the tricks up his book.'

It's unlike Davies not to hector, but in fairness he usually lets it pass without comment, although you can picture a Bazza eyebrow arching like a frightened cat.

It's when Bright the fact-checker swings into action, however, that Bazza feels duty-bound to shout 'stop'. Cue memorable exchanges like this:

Brighty: Both of Celtic's scorers are English.
Bazza: I'll have to correct you there, Mark, John Hartson is Welsh.
Brighty: OK – English-based.

It certainly would be wise for Brighty to master the basics of his trade before graduating to Commentating 102: the metaphor:

'Stuart McCall is trying to thread a needle through a haystack there.'

Credit where it's due, however. Brighty is responsible for one of modern football's very finest quotes. Spotting a stricken exhibitionist during a Premiership clash between Portsmouth and Villa, he remarked:

'He signals to the bench with his groin.'

☆ David Pleat

In a nutshell: He's done just about every job there is to do in football.

Gaffta Panel Verdict: He's committed just about every gaffe there is to commit in football.

If these awards were being distributed for sartorial faux pas and undignified japery, Pleaty would certainly be included in the Best Gaffer category. After all, his frenzied hop-skip-and-jump routine across Maine Road in a beige suit and off-white loafers after Luton Town avoided relegation in 1983 remains a landmark moment in the rich history of managerial lunacy.

Even when it comes to gaffes, David's handsome back catalogue is divided pretty evenly between post-match managerial buffoonery and idiosyncratic ITV co-commentary. However, since his recent record suggests even including Pleaty in the same sentence as the words 'gaffer' and 'best' might be an act of unprecedented generosity, co-commentator Pleat it is. And here are the top verbal equivalents of his garish attire.

Pleaty's approach to player underperformance was callous:
'If there are any managers out there with a bottomless pit, I'm sure that they would be interested in these two Russians.'

But he certainly understood what made a player tick:
'There's Thierry Henry, exploding like the French train that he is.'

And player bonding was never a problem in Pleat's teams:
'Our central defenders, Doherty and Anthony Gardner, were fantastic and I told them that when they go to bed tonight they should think of each other.'

Pleaty was always a huge fan of dexterity:
'Stoichkov is pointing at the bench with his eyes.'

A man famed for his compassion, he sensitively noted that the Champions League clash for which Gérard Houllier made his comeback after illness was . . .
'. . . not a game for the faint-hearted.'

Pleat's managerial philosophy was simple:
'A game is not won until it is lost.'

But Pleat the co-commentator had a few refinements to make to that philosophy:

'Eighty per cent of teams who score first in matches go on to win them. But they may draw some. Or occasionally lose . . .'

And Pleat in neither guise took anything for granted:

'Had we not got that second goal, I think the score might have been different. I'm not sure.'

Mind you, few commentators describe a goal quite like Pleaty:

'He hits it into the corner of the net as straight as a nut.'

Speaking of nuts, when latterly reincarnated as a Director of Football, Pleat knew the qualities he wanted in a manager and one out of three wasn't enough for Glenn Hoddle:

'The man we want has to fit a certain profile. Is he a top coach? Would the players respect him? Is he a nutcase?'

☆ Trevor Brooking

In a nutshell: Football's foremost pipe-and-slippers man.
Gaffta Panel Verdict: Content-free speaking style only occasionally makes for comedy. Management's the place for Trev, if he can make the effort.

Perhaps you'd be so kind as to participate in a short test? Actually, not so much a test as an experiment. A scientific exercise in guffological analysis. It shouldn't be too painful. Ready? OK, examine if you will ten random excerpts from the legendary co-commentary career of Sir Trev. Study them carefully; there will be questions later.

1. **'If you're going to score one goal or less, you're not going to get your victories.'**

2. **'Merseyside derbys usually last 90 minutes and I'm sure today's won't be any different.'**

3. 'Unfortunately, we don't get a second chance. We've already played them twice.'

4. 'He looks as though he's been playing for England all his international career.'

5. 'You're always going to be struggling if you haven't got a left foot.'

6. 'You shouldn't go behind in the early minutes because then you have to chase the game.'

7. 'That could have been his second yellow card . . . if he'd already got his first one, of course . . .'

8. 'The managerial vacancy at the club remains vacant.'

9. 'He is like an English equivalent of Teddy Sheringham.'

10. 'Historically, the host nations do well in Euro 2000.'

OK, wake up, now for the science bit. You may need to perform some complex calculations, so by all means get a calculator if you need one.

With careful reference to the above statements, allocate Trev points based on the following criteria.

One point for each slice of valuable tactical insight from England's Director of Football Development.

Two points for each little-known entertaining fact imparted by Trev.

Three points for each profundity.

Seven points for each statement that is likely to have helped the viewer better understand the confusing business that is association football.

Twenty points for each decisive uncategorical pronouncement from Trevor.

OK, we've already made up our minds about Trevor, so this test is actually all about you. Depending on the points total you calculated, our team of trained guffologists suggest you belong in one of two categories.
1 to 231: You are a kind and generous soul, perhaps a little too sensitive to be reading mocking, unkind publications about footballing personalities who, after all, are only doing their best. We suggest you put this book down and go for a nice walk.
Zero: You're spot on, mate.

Yes, Trevor 'Trev' Brooking is the Switzerland of football commentary – Motty's bet-hedging sidekick for whom no decision is too small to be avoided. A co-commentator whose fear of getting it wrong has destroyed any chance of him ever getting it right.

To be fair, he's done well to have had such a distinguished career in the game after a complicated birth atop a large wooden fence. And to this day, he somehow convinces outwardly sensible men like Gary Lineker to seek from him, time and again, pertinent information. Naturally, each and every time, they're disappointed:

Lineker: Trevor Brooking is in the Sapporo Bowl. What's it like, Trevor?
Brooking: Welllllll, it's a bowl shape, Gary.

The trademark 'wellllllll' – sometimes extended into a 'wellllll yeaaa knowwwwww' is a vital component of the Brooking broadcasting toolkit – providing a helpful buffer following a question, during which Trev can compose a suitably non-committal answer:

'A bad miss, Trevor?'
'Wellllllll yeaaa knooowwwww, John. He should have felt he probably scored then.'

And yet, for all his woolly waffling on the telly, Trevor's double stint as West Ham caretaker gaffer showcased an entirely different side to the man. Calm and decisive, he struck an impressive figure in the Hammers' dugout. It made us think again – rummage once more through the Brooking guff CV. Was there more to the man than fence sitting?

We suppose, from time to time, there have been hints of a sense of humour and – Heaven forfend! – the odd acerbic remark during an uneventful game:

'It's end to end stuff, but from side to side.'

A hint of malevolence maybe:

'Fortunately, Paul Scholes' injury wasn't as bad as we'd hoped for.'

And a keen eye for a serious medical condition:

'No, I saw him kick the bucket over there which suggests he's not going to be able to continue.'

'Simon Davies has had a few injuries. Maybe he wasn't fully foot.'

Overall, perhaps it's only fitting that Trev should become only the second guffster whose achievements have been recognised with a knighthood. And true to form, he reacted to the award in the unique style with which he built a career:

'I've had a fantastic lot of two wonderful messages.'
Welllllllllll!

WINNER

☆ Graham Taylor

In a nutshell: In everything he turns his hand to, he bestrides the fine line between comedic genius and just being a bit of a clown.
Gaffta Panel Verdict: This man's strongest suit is deliberate humour, funnily enough.

'Hey! Hey! Tell your pal that he's just cost me my job.'
One of the last haunted cries of Graham Taylor's reign as England gaffer, while he was chasing a helpless linesman down the Rotterdam touchline after the referee failed to send off Ronald Koeman for upending David Platt as he ran through on goal. Yes, that Ronald Koeman, who, naturally, went on to score the free kick that ensured that England wouldn't be going anywhere near the 1994 World Cup finals.

In reality, poor old Taylor would soon lose much more than his job. Already christened 'Turniphead' by the Fleet Street wags, the Channel 4 documentary *An Impossible Job*, which focused on Taylor's management through that qualifying campaign, would strip him of the remainder of his dignity and coin the classic managerial phrase of the time: 'Do I not like that!'

In the programme, Taylor's increasing desperation – and sidekick Phil Neal's unrelenting sycophancy – was vividly exposed during another abject England showing in Poland, where that great philosophical puzzle 'Can we not knock it?' got its first airing:

Des Walker knocks a misplaced pass to John Barnes:
Taylor: 'Ooooh, f**king . . . Do I not like that!'

Poland win the ball, break downfield and score:
Taylor: What a f**king ball. What a ball, eh, from Des to Barnesy. What a f**king . . . It was our possession.

Phil Neal: I know.

Taylor: It was from our free kick. We've come square, and the ball . . . Des and Barnesy, eh? F**king ball, eh? You can talk till you're f**king blue in the face, can't you?

Phil Neal: Yes, boss.

The game kicks off again:

Taylor: Come on. Bigger, bigger.

Another misplaced pass:

Taylor: We've done that f**king . . . CAN WE NOT KNOCK IT? They've done everything that we told them not to do. Everything that we told them not to do.

And the full misery of the Dutch denouement was compelling, if heartbreaking, viewing:

Taylor: Linesman, linesman, what sort of thing is happening here? You know it, you know it, don't you? Absolutely disgraceful.

Linesman mutters something:

Taylor: Linesman, linesman, that's a disgrace . . . Hell's Bells!

Koeman hasn't even scored the free kick yet. In the gantry, Brian Moore is first to cotton on to what's about to happen:

'He's going to flip one. He's going to flip one. HE'S GOING TO FLIP ONE.'

Koeman has scored:

Taylor: I'll tell you, they don't f**king deserve it. F**king. That is absolutely shocking.

Businesslike for a moment:

Taylor: We'll have to get Wrighty on shortly.

Phil Neal: We'll have to give Wrighty a go.

Taylor turns his attention once more to the beleaguered linesman:
'You know we've been cheated, don't you?'

Linesman motions him back to his technical area:
'I have a metre. I have a metre. You know. It's all right.'

Linesman is getting fed up. Goes to report Taylor, who pleads for mercy:
'I won't say anything else. Come on, don't. But I'm allowed to stay in the metre.'

Linesman lets him off with a warning. However, the peace bond is soon broken:
'Even if he doesn't see it as a penalty, he has to go. You know that. I know you know it, so . . . And then the fella scores the free kick.'

A sudden outbreak of bonhomie from Taylor:
'You can't say anything. I know you can't say anything. I know that.'

Again it's short-lived:
'But, you see, at the end of the day, I get the sack. Will you say to the fella, the referee has got me the sack? Thank him ever so much for that, won't you?'

Although he worked again in the game – and with a degree of success too – Taylor's reputation has never quite recovered. Like David Pleat nowadays, the work of Taylor the co-commentator has rather surpassed that of Taylor the gaffer. After all, no one has yet superimposed a root vegetable on his shoulders after a slipshod turn in the gantry. It may, however, be simply a matter of time:

'In football, time and space are the same thing.'
Graham's special turnip continuum puts Einstein and co. in their places.

'Well, it's a love–hate relationship and he loves me.'
Graham Taylor speaks glowingly of his working relationship with Villa chairman, Doug Ellis.

'Shearer could be at 100 per cent fitness, but not peak fitness.'
One of those managers who always looked for 110 per cent.

'Sometimes it's very hard to follow what would have happened and sometimes it's hard to follow what has happened.'
. . . and sometimes its very hard to follow Graham Taylor.

'To be really happy, we must throw our hearts over the bar and hope that our bodies will follow.'
As Phil Neal might say, 'That's right, boss.'

'Very few of us have any idea whatsoever of what life is like living in a goldfish bowl – except, of course, for those of us who are goldfish.'
Once a turnip, now reincarnated as a goldfish. Suppose they're roughly the same colour.

'I'd never allow myself to let myself call myself a coward.'
Nor would we prevent ourselves from stopping ourselves calling you a guff merchant.

'What a clinical finish. That's got nothing to do with his haircut at all. That's footballing ability.'
Hard-but-fair Graham scuppers any chance Clint Mathis's barber had of claiming an assist for the USA's goal against South Korea.

'I sometimes wished I'd been shot . . . though it never came to that . . . nor should it.'
Musing on his time as England manager, Graham lectures a chastened public on the rights and wrongs of football manager assassination.

'The thing about coming to watch football in this part of the world is it makes you realise what a world game it is.'
Two-thirds of the way through the World Cup, Graham eventually cottons on to what's been happening for the last three weeks.

'There may have been a problem with the wall of two or two and a half players.'
Graham reveals that at least one English player lost his head before a Portugal goal.

'Nothing that UEFA or FIFA do surprises me any more, and I'm very surprised this has not been sorted out long in advance.'
Nothing more surprising than the element of surprise.

'He knows they've got to score three goals. They know they've got to score three goals. What more can you say?'
Graham showcases the tactical awareness he brought to the England job.

'That's a goal, isn't it, but what a good save!'
It wasn't and it was.

'I think what would help the Ecuadorian side is if they could get a glimpse of the possibility of scoring a goal.'
Do you reckon, Graham?

'Their hospitality has been fantastic and a good example to many other countries. I can't think of one . . .'
Probably better that way, Graham.

LINGUISTIC ACHIEVEMENT AWARD: RON ATKINSON

THE GAFFTA AWARDS

'I am not a racist, I am an idiot.'
The plea of a broken Ron after his ugly diatribe against Marcel Desailly became the biggest commentating gaffe of all.

It's a poor excuse. Mainly because Ron is patently not an idiot. Perhaps instead, we can offer an alternative get-out: that Ron's greatest mistake was reverting to the primitive language he'd long left behind. For, normally, all the gold in the world can't persuade him to communicate in English.

Until the fateful night of 20 April 2004 in Monaco, Ron had no truck with the crude dialect that led him so sadly astray. Instead, he has toiled for years in the hot Marbella sun to construct a language all of his own. It's an inspiring, magical lingo that became Ron's signature throughout his legendary partnership with Clive.

DangerHere.com was the first to call it Ronglish and it seems to have stuck. An exhaustive dissection would require a book of its own, but at the heart of the language lies an ingenious lexicon of terms that have become the lingua franca of the gantry.

He might have fallen from grace. He might never make it back to a commentary box and perhaps he shouldn't. Nevertheless, his language will live on. We present a selection of it here.

AN A TO Z OF RONGLISH

AIR MILES:

Of course he's not a long-ball man, but Ron is rarely more chuffed than when he sees a spectacular pass delivered accurately over distance. And such is the stockpile of *air miles* the big man has amassed trekking south for tan top-ups, he has no hesitation distributing a generous allocation among European football's playmakers.

Ron might say:

'Tell you what, Clive, Beckham's been picking out those runs for fun all night, but that ball travelled so far it should have had *air miles*.'

AMUSEMENT ARCADE:

Much as he likes a player to have a trick 'in his locker', suspicious Ron is wary of the gent who sells one *lollipop* too many at the expense of 'knocking it out of his feet' and 'having a dig'. Such dilettantes are dismissed as *amusement arcades*.

Although still very much a recent classic, Ron was expected to bring this favourite into the technology age by making Robbie Keane the first Sony PlayStation to play in the Premiership.

Ron might say:

'All right, the big Nigerian's a crowd pleaser, Clive, but by 'eck he can be a bit of an *amusement arcade*. Go on, son, give it the full gun!'

ARRIVE:

It can't be easy single-handedly shaping the evolution of your own language. Sometimes Ron gets tired; he struggles for inspiration. It's times like these that he turns to that more primitive means of human communication, English. In an inspired bid to develop the ideal description of a perfectly timed run into the penalty area, Ron cunningly transforms the verb, 'to arrive', into a noun. As usual, it works a treat. Another triumph for Ron that makes a monkey of those boys at Oxford who look after the dictionaries. You know he's right, lads, get it sorted.

Ron might say:

'Keane's pinged that in the gully, Giggsy's faced one to the first post, Forlan's missed out, but look at the *arrive* from the little ginger fella. One–zero.'

BLATTER:

In a grand tribute to FIFA president Sepp, a man of similar hue to himself, Ron has coined this, his latest term for a powerfully struck shot. As with much of his versatile vocab, *blatter* works equally well as a verb or a noun. However, in most cases, a *blatter* is not recognised unless Ron has issued the vigorous attacker in question with a personal invitation to shoot, or at least had a timely premonition.

Ron might say:

'Go on, big man, give it the full gun . . . TELL YOU WHAT, Clive, he has absolutely *blattered* it!'

Or he might say:

'I had a funny feeling the little fella might just trigger one, Clive, but that is a *blatter*! One–zero.'

BONKING:

Ruud Gullit's not the only one who can appreciate a bit of sexy football, you know. Nothing gets Ron in the mood better than the sight of a lively footballer haring unhindered down the wing.

Don't go thinking the big man's easy, though. It takes a certain Latin quality to get Ron's pulse racing. A pasty Irishman like John O'Shea will simply go 'marching down the flank'.

Ron might say:

'You might have thought Bayern would have read the

script, Clive. As soon as Zidane goes inside, Roberto Carlos just goes *bonking* off down the wing.'

BUDDY HOLLY:

The single most controversial and debated term in the lexicon, source of a bitter and perhaps irreconcilable split between two factions of Ronglish scholars. 'Buddygate,' they tended to call it.

Original Ronglish teachings provided a rather disappointingly straightforward explanation, insisting the *Buddy Holly* was simply rhyming slang for volley. So-and-so goes *bonking* down the right, knocks one to the *second post* and such-and-such catches it clean on the *Buddy Holly*. End of story. Or so it appeared.

Ronglish conservatives hadn't, however, reckoned on a team of crack Ugandan guffologists who produced a startling alternative theory after poring over almost a million hours of sparkling co-commentary.

In these remarkable findings, it is suggested that the *Buddy Holly* finds daring Ron, in one of his rather less politically correct moments, evoking the memory of the unfortunate crooner's airborne demise to paint a picture of any sharp descent to earth.

Furthermore, in an ironic twist, it is suggested that many of the charlatans whose tumbles Ron has likened to Holly's emerge gleefully unscathed after their dramatic plunges – in marked contrast to Buddy's fatal freefall. Robert Pires, hang your head.

The truth about the *Buddy Holly* may lie somewhere in between. Perhaps having tried out the less PC variation one Tuesday night when a bunch of Eastern European drama queens pitched up at Old Trafford, Ron was swiftly talked out of it by Clive, who apparently does a mean version of Peggy Sue.

Whatever happened, the suggestion that Ron might have added to Dennis Bergkamp's problems by giving him a new-found fear of diving looks to be nonsense. For one thing, the Dutchman continues to tumble like a girl whenever the mood takes him.

Ron might say:
'He's got no right to even hit the target there, Clive, but to be fair, he's bought a ticket and caught that bang on the *Buddy Holly*.'

Revisionist Ron might say:
'Tell you what, Clive, I know the lad's got a nudge early doors, but Pires has gone down like *Buddy Holly* there.'

BURSTING BLOOD-VESSELS:

Back in the '80s, Ron greeted news of his sacking as Manchester United gaffer by enquiring politely of Martin Edwards if he could still use the Old Trafford gym for his Friday night five-a-side.

Sadly, time waits for no man, and nowadays Doctor Ron equates any sudden exertion of physical effort with an inevitable and painful need for *blood-vessels* to burst. Perhaps the Spanish sun isn't the only key to his distinctive pigmentation.

Ron was, of course, a midfielder in his day, so, naturally, it is primarily to those who man the engine room that he attributes this debilitating condition. In particular, any midfield man with a penchant for late runs into the box can expect to sunder at least half a dozen *blood-vessels* during an average 90 minutes.

Ron might say:
'To be fair, Clive, full marks to Big Heskey for letting that bounce off him, but, tell you what, the boy Gerrard has absolutely burst *blood-vessels* to make the *arrive*. One–zero.'

CHANGE BALL:

Ron's love for the beautiful game has been a long-running affair and he has never let the magic die. What helps is that Ron has never lost his capacity to be surprised by events on the field of play.

The occurrence of a *change ball* is one such moment, and it never fails to tickle Ron pink. The *change ball* takes place when a player cunningly chooses not to pass the ball in the direction he's facing, but in another direction entirely – momentarily outfoxing the opposition in the process and perhaps even switching the point of attack. Importantly, the pass cannot actually play a teammate in on goal as a *change ball* achieving this result automatically earns a *spotter's badge*.

Ron might say:

'Parlour's lobbed him a bit of an ugly one, but the big French fella's given them "the eyes" and knocked a lovely *change ball*. Shame Pires wasn't in the *Wide Awake Club*.'

CHEATING POSITION:

It's often debated whether it was the gantry's goldenest geezer who first invented 'the hole', that twilight zone normally populated by gloved *amusement arcades* who just don't fancy challenging for headers with the centre-halves. If it was, Ron cannot be best pleased to hear every Tom, Dick and Mark Bright get the shovels out nowadays any time a lazy frontman can't be arsed getting in the box.

This may be why he's had to go to extra lengths to define this mythical role.

Ron might say:

'Tell you what, Clive, I don't think the little ginger fella's enjoying the attention of these two outhouses. He's begun to drift a little . . . taken up the *cheating position*, if you like.'

COURSE AND DISTANCE:

OK, where do you think Ron got this one?

1. From the marine terminology for measuring the actual and radial distance between two known points. Note to seafaring enthusiasts: the measurement starting point cannot be a pole.

2. Down at the racecourse, where the initials 'C' and 'D'

appear beside choice nags on the meeting form guide, kindly alerting punters that (a) the horse in question has previously triumphed on this COURSE and (b) has done the business elsewhere over the equivalent DISTANCE.

Yeah, you're probably right. Especially as Ron's *course and distance* is used to describe players who've been round a while, put their medals on the table and 'seen it all before, Clive'.

Ron might say:

'Sir Alex thinks a lot of young Fletcher, but I just wonder if he should have opted for Nicky Butt to play the frontscreen role. I know he's not in the best of form, but he's got *course and distance* at this level.'

CROWD SCENE:

Ron always likes to give it a bit of Hollywood, but this movie reference evokes sad memories of the big man's alleged failure to cut the mustard as a terrified villager in the first Indiana Jones film. Nowadays, every packed goalmouth reminds Ron of what might have been. Still, the silver screen's loss is comic co-commentary's gain.

Ron might say:

'Little Wright-Phillips has loaded that in the mixer again, but the way Liverpool are defending, it's a [sob] *crowd scene* in there.'

CRUELTY TO DEFENDERS ACT:

'You just can't legislate for pace like that,' you'll often hear Clive and his likes conclude, as a pair of 'lightning slow' centre-halves trail in the wake of a pacy frontman. Yet again, these fellows have underestimated the resourcefulness of Ron, who has drafted his very own constitution to cater for just such eventualities.

Justice Atkinson might say:

'Tell you what, Clive, wouldn't you like to see Henry and van Nistelrooy in the same side? Mind you, that might be banned under the *Cruelty to Defenders Act*.'

CURLY FINGER:

Ron loves nothing more than a tactical substitution. First, of course, he has to call it. At the slightest hint of activity on the benches, Ron will use his managerial nous and renowned ability to lean out of the gantry to see who's warming up, to give it the full gun with loads of 'Tell you what, Clive, he might just pull off the big frontman and get more bodies in the engine room'-type guff.

Then, when the switch is actually made, Ron is quick to register his amusement at the departing player's misfortune.

Ron might say:

'Yep, I was right, Clive, Big Heskey's getting the *curly finger* all right.'

DOUBLE TANDEM:

Ron has shown more than once that he appreciates the value of an understanding partner. So it's no surprise that this description of a pair of players who work well together is a firm favourite.

Although a *double tandem* usually refers to players playing in the same position or part of the pitch – for example a pair of central defenders, midfielders or strikers – spontaneous *double tandems* can occur anywhere when players from different positions link up well. The one small problem with this fine concoction is that, numerically speaking, a *double tandem* would contain four players rather than two. But it would be churlish to dampen the great man's enthusiasm by mentioning this.

Always looking to innovate, Ron has recently refined the *double tandem* to allow for more precise definitions. Thus we have seen the advent of the *double left-handed tandem*, an asymmetrical axis where both parties favour their left sides. Of course, Ron rarely gets to witness the *double left-handed tandem* as left-footed footballers have been extinct in England for five million years.

'Tell you what, Clive, the little winger's more of a jinker than a flier, but that *double left-handed tandem* with the big full-back's gonna take some stopping, if you like.'

DROPPINGS:

Never truly a fan of the long-ball percentage game – where aimless 'fighting balls' are loaded on top of 'big lighthouses' – Ron rather betrays his prejudice with this striker knockdowns as excrement theory.

Ron might say:

'There's only two ways of playing against Big Duncan. If you're a big lighthouse yourself, contest every ball with him. If not, let him have it and pick up his *droppings.'*

EARLY DOORS:

Not, of course, a Ron original, the term coming either from the theatre or the licensed trade, depending on the Ronglish scholar whose homework you copy. Given Ron's notorious thirst for champagne, perhaps the latter is more likely.

Wherever it came from, Ron has to take much of the credit for *early doors* firmly establishing itself in the vocabulary of any football man worth his salt, and indeed for introducing this completely useless phrase to most of the English-speaking world.

For *early doors*, of course, is actually that most unusual of abbreviations, one that is double the length of the word it attempts to truncate. A somewhat uneconomical alternative for the times when the word 'early' on its own somehow doesn't quite get across the earliness of a situation.

It might not be Ron's finest hour, but it certainly picks up the Best Adaptation From an Original Screenplay gong.

Ron might say:

'Well, United went one down *early doors*, but all credit, those four penalties certainly got them back in it.'

EASY-OASY:

The array of jewels regularly adorning Ron's person is testament indeed to the big man's willingness to mix and match. And a school of thought exists that this commonly used piece of Ronglish is, in fact, a cunning amalgamation of the words easy-going and lazy. And what Ron shall put together, let no man pull apart. So from here on in, WWF wrestler turned occasional footballer Emile Heskey shall be known in these quarters as nothing else.

Ron might say:

'Funnily enough, Clive. I've thought Heskey's been a bit *easy-oasy* all night, but that was a *stick-on*. The big feller really should have notched.'

FACER:

Simple yet ingenious. A *facer* is an out-swinging cross, usually executed from somewhere close to the end line and driven across the face of goal. Or, as Ron so often puts it: 'the kind of ball goalkeepers and defenders hate dealing with'.

In familiar Ronglish style, this works just as well as a verb, so dextrous wide men will always look to '*face* balls into dangerous areas'. Better still, in an ideal world the *facer* should be propelled right down the 'corridor of uncertainty'.

Ron might say:

'To be fair, Giggsy has *faced* a beauty into the zone, and normally you can hang your hat on the big Dutch fella from there.'

FLYING MACHINE:

Luddites still credit the Wright brothers with the first significant air-travel milestone. Of course, they overlook Ron's groundbreaking work in converting a lively wide man into the very first human aircraft. In fact, ever since his own turn of pace was amply replaced by a turn of phrase, Ron often used his microphone and headset to seek clearance from air traffic control every time a speedy winger knocked it out of his feet and turned on the turbo.

Ron might say:

'They've set their stall out to keep it tight at the back, dog the ball in midfield, and get it down the *gullies* for the *flying machine* to chase.'

FOR FUN:

Ron's philosophy on life is simple: do what you enjoy. Hence champagne-quaffing, sunbed-lounging and gold-shopping feature heavily in any Atkinson itinerary. Therefore, when Ron sees a footballer doing something over and over, he can only presume the lad is enjoying himself.

Though many football pundits seem to be joyless fellows – particularly former Irish internationals with surnames like Stapleton, Houghton or Bonner – all these chaps know how to let their hair down of a Tuesday night in a club. Hence *for fun* has become a commentating staple and is particularly popular with Andy 'Dancing Shoes' Gray.

Ron might say:

'Tell you what, Clive, the little fellow on the left is going past Lauren *for fun* tonight.'

FULL GUN:

Ron's gangsta tendencies come to the fore with this succinct description of a powerful shot. Curiously, this is normally used only when, despite the fullness of the gun, the brave custodian manages to thwart the violent assault on goal.

Ron might say:

'Blimey, Parlour's given that the *full gun*, but it's gone straight down Walker's throat.'

GLASS MOUNTAIN:

Whereas a theatrical foreign player might throw himself to the ground like *Buddy Holly*, a Premiership side packed with temperamental foreign types who don't like it up 'em may experience an even sharper plummet when the going gets tough after Easter, finding themselves sliding down Ron's mythical *glass mountain* towards the relegation zone.

Ron might say:

'A few weeks ago, Des, Middlesbrough looked to be cruising. But after a performance like that, they could find themselves sliding down the *glass mountain* if they're not careful.'

GONE EMPTY:

Always a man keen to be let off the leash, Ron gets particularly excited when he sees a player given a bit of latitude by opposing defenders. If the escapee in question is a bit of an *amusement arcade* and Ron thinks there's no immediate danger, he may content himself with an 'in acres'. But if he fancies the unfettered attacker may give it the *full gun*, it's got to be *gone empty*.

It probably goes without saying, but a player who picks out a teammate that has *gone empty* invariably earns a *spotter's badge*.

Ron might say:

'Tell you what, Clive, shame the little ginger fella's not in the *Wide Awake Club* there, 'cos if he could have dug one out, Forlan was "in acres" and van Nistelrooy had *gone empty* at the *second post*.'

GULLY:

A mythical land of much prosperity situated roughly between the centre-halves and a full-back.

On more prosaic European nights, or maybe on *The Premiership*, Ron might have settled for calling it 'the channel'. Whatever, the *gully* is the first port of call for any player a little unsure of what he should do next.

If in doubt, frontmen should attack the gully, wide men ought to run down the gullies and much fortune and favour shall be heaped on he who 'knocks one into the *gully* for the little runaway striker to chase'.

Ron might say:

'Tell you what, Clive, it's stick or bust for Chelsea now, let's get the *trumpets* out and attack them down the *gullies*.'

HAILING A TAXI:

There's nothing more likely to cost you a goal than when an excitable goalkeeper forgets you're defending a 91st-minute corner and hares out of his goal with an arm aloft looking for a ride into town.

Ron might say:

'Tell you what, Clive, this fella's normally Mr Dependability between the sticks, but he's come out there like he's *hailing a taxi*.'

HOLLYWOOD BALL:

Throughout David Beckham's United career, he was challenged only by sometime teammate and full-time *amusement arcade* Juan Sebastian Veron as the undisputed king of the *Hollywood Ball*, an ambitious pass that practically craves the award of a *spotter's badge*. The problem with the *Hollywood Ball* is that it regularly ignores the five-yard *facer* that would have left the little ginger fella standing empty after a great little *arrive*. Not to be confused with a *change ball*, though these can also harbour some LA ambitions.

Ron might say:

'I just wonder, Clive, if Beckham shouldn't get hold of it and put a threat on, instead of launching those *Hollywood Balls* towards the big Brazilian feller.'

INSTALMENTS:

Fast-moving Ron is particularly sceptical of the beautiful game's less lively protagonists. The poet of the gantry has a host of barbed dismissals in his locker, but 'in *instalments*' is reserved for displays of ground-breaking slowness.

Instalments has become extremely popular with the kind of pundit who might also suggest that wingers go down 'like a sack of spuds'. Stand up Jim Beglin.

However, the whole slowness area is one on which Ron had to keep working, if only to beat off competition from the classic Eamon Dunphy description of a tardily diving goalie – 'He's gone down like a roll of lino.'

Ron might say:

'Tell you what, I know Big Dichio's lightning slow but he was JCBing it there. Reckon I've seen the *QE2* turn faster and the big lad's gone in the box in *instalments*.'

LITTLE EYEBROWS:

The rich visual content of the Ronglish vocabulary is showcased with this delightful description of a glancing backward header. Often used in conjunction with *second post*.

While much of Ron's language has spread throughout the football world, nobody has yet attempted to pull off the *eyebrows* – possibly because of the sheer degree of difficulty.

It's likely also that Andy Gray – a chief Ronglish plagiarist – has been deterred only because he can't get out of his mind the anything-but-little eyebrows sported by Richard Keys.

Ron might have said in 1989:

'It's gone in there, *little eyebrows* from Bouldy and there's big Tone steaming in at the *second post*.'

Ron might say in 2004, despite Arsenal not having scored in this fashion for several centuries:

'The Arsenal are great in these positions, Clive. Just needs

a *little eyebrows* at the first post and Keown will be looking for an ugly one round the back.'

LOLLIPOP:

Excitable Ron's description of a popular football skill usually performed by a 'tricky' winger.

It is suspected that this Ronglish classic may owe something to the lollipop stick/trick cockney rhyming slang staple, although an early form of the term can be traced to the early '60s when Ron's gaffer at Oxford United, Arthur Turner, greeted Ron's ill-advised attempt to dribble his way out of trouble with the cutting – and confusing – rebuke: 'You're nothing but a dustman's lollipop.'

Anyhow, in Ron's eyes the *lollipop* involves the trickster waving one or both feet over a stationary football, much to the bemusement of the onlooking Jamie Carragher.

Ron has said:

'Denilson's given it about *20 lollipops* there, Clive.'

MILKY (AKA LEAFY):

You suspect Ron takes his coffee black, particularly after a tough night on the sunbed, quaffing champers from a gold goblet. When you throw in the likely mid-morning caviar-on-toast with a side order of chips, it's understandable that a gentleman of such iron constitution might be a little suspicious of the lily-livered late drinker.

Thus, Ron describes as *milky* any player – invariably foreign, usually an *amusement arcade* – he suspects might be somewhat lacking in what Johnny Giles would call 'moral courage'. Stick a *reducer early doors* into a *milky* opponent, and he'll wander disconsolately into the *cheating position*, stick his hands on his hips and go *easy-oasy* for the rest of the night.

Ron might say:

'Just maybe, Clive, if United can put a tempo on, I just wonder if Ballack isn't a little bit *milky* in there.'

PLAYING FROM AMNESIA:

Somewhat surprisingly, given his own gainful employment through his golden years, ageist Ron is quick to have a pop at veterans he reckons may well have outlived their usefulness.

Maybe it's just that most pundits have yet to experience much in the way of memory loss – Bobby Robson doesn't do much of that type of work – but this one hasn't taken off. In an ironic twist, Ron may well have forgotten it himself as we haven't heard it for many a year.

Ron might say:

'The little ginger fella's done him no favours with that ball, but, tell you what, Clive, Blanc looks like he's *playing from amnesia* out there.'

PLAYING STATUES:

Watching Arsenal in Europe frequently caused Ron to fondly recall the fourth great love of his life (behind champers, gold and sunbeds), the timeless art of mime. Frequently startled by the sight of assembled rear Gunners helplessly admiring some Johnny Foreigner waltzing through on goal, Ron often concluded that the hapless defenders in question must have temporarily acquired some part-time work as still mime artists. Given Sol Campbell's professed theatrical bent, he may well have had a point.

In a subtle variation on *playing statues*, Ron sometimes simply accused an *easy-oasy* back four of 'playing standing still'.

Ron might say:

'To be fair, the big Norwegian has put a threat on all night, but Arsenal are *playing statues* at the back.'

REBOUND POSITION:

Not quite the *cheating position*, that favoured hiding place of *amusement arcades* everywhere. No, the rebound position is the one that David Ginola devoted a career to perfecting.

Normally the preserve of wide men – either jinkers or fliers – the position essentially involves sticking your hands on your hips and going *easy-oasy* as the opposing full-back starts creeping in a bid to bolster the attack.

Then when the move goes pear-shaped thanks to Phil Neville, you can receive the ball standing empty in acres. The boy Figo has got this one down.

Ron might say:

'Tell you what, Clive, this lot are definitely get-at-able. Giggsy's been hanging about in the *rebound position* and if Neville can bomb a big diagonal, I back the Welsh wizard to snaffle one.'

REDUCER:

Though not a violent man, even Ron accepts the need for a bit of argy-bargy every now and again to put the frighteners on an opponent. This classic Ronglish refers to the type of 'introductory' challenges defenders like to dish out to potential *amusement arcades* early on in a game.

Ron has said:

'Babbel might want to put a few *reducers* into Pires early on.'

SECOND POST:

Where less helpful pundits would talk about the 'far post', Ron – never one to discriminate against the uninitiated – thoughtfully provides a clue as to the location of this post to those not familiar with the rudiments of goalpost construction.

Shamefully, ne'er-do-wells like Gray and Parry are appropriating Ron's mathematical approach to post identification. So much so that Ron has been forced to up the ante by clearing up the whole near post issue as well. First post it is then.

Ron might say:

'. . . and nobody's picked up Cole at the *second post*. Shame about the finish.'

SOUND OF THE TRUMPETS:

It's not widely known that Ron apparently keeps a host of model armies in the cellar of one his Marbella retreats, regularly restaging many of the world's most famous battles. His favourite tactic is, of course, a good old-fashioned cavalry charge and this often comes to mind during commentary when a team makes a bold tactical switch.

Funnily enough, Ron already seems keen to abbreviate this one to simply *trumpets*. Sensibly, however, he caters for new Ronglish students by issuing the occasional reminder as to why said *trumpets* are being produced:

'It's not time for United to get the *trumpets* out yet . . . so they can go to the sound of them, that is.'

Ron might say:

'Tell you what, Peter. I think they're going to pull off the little full-back, stick the big man up the front and go to the *sound of the trumpets*.'

SPOTTER'S BADGE:

A metaphorical prize awarded by Ron when a player he likes makes a perceptive pass.

Clearly most football commentators are less familiar with ornithological parlance than the tanned wordsmith, because *spotter's badge* remains largely a Ron special.

However, recent shameless plagiarism by Andy Gray, who once awarded a *spotter's badge* to co-commentator Brian Marwood on *Monday Night Football*, suggests the coveted prize will soon be handed out by all and sundry.

Ron might say:

'*Spotter's badge* for Scholesy to put Forlan clear. Shame about the finish.'

STICK-ON:

One of Ronglish's more versatile components, the *stick-on* is a handy label Ron affixes to any event his expert eye deems to be a foregone conclusion.

Never a man to drop a monkey down the bookies, Ron knows a sure thing when he sees it. Thus, for instance, United at home to Sturm Graz would be an 'absolute *stick-on*' in Ron's book.

Similarly, the big gold-horse declares any goal-scoring opportunity where you can hang your hat on the frontman registering a *stick-on*. Indeed, it is kindly Ron's very lack of discrimination in this regard that causes many a *stick-on* to become a real 'rick'.

Ron might say:

'To be fair to Yorkie, he's done his little trick, fizzed a *facer* into the zone. And tell you what, Coley has missed an absolute *stick-on* there.'

WATCHING CARTOONS:

Very much a fan of the sun, Ron's devotion to perfecting his distinctive Tangoman colouring leaves little time for sitting around watching television. However, when he does have a few minutes to spare, Ron loves to catch up with his favourite *Tom and Jerry* episodes. Hence, when the big man witnesses an outlandish act on the field of play, he reckons the protagonists involved have also been taking their cues from his heroes.

Ron might say:

'Tell you what, Clive, he's been *watching cartoons* if he thinks he can beat Barthez from there.'

WIDE AWAKE CLUB:

Child-at-heart Ron recalls the – mercifully brief – glory days of would-be entertainer Timmy Mallett to rebuke players who react less than brightly when presented with a goal-scoring opportunity.

No harm in trying, Ron, but no comeback beckons for the former breakfast-time irritant. Still, as an avid follower of the Mallett career, Ron is expected to utter any day now: '. . . great strike but just an itsy bitsy teeny weeny bit wide'.

Ron might say:

'Tell you what, Clive, the little ginger fella's done wonders there to ghost in and pop that off. Just a shame the little Norwegian's not in the *Wide Awake Club* tonight.'

THE PLAYERS' AWARD

Professional footballers have evolved splendidly over the decades. As a group, they are now expert in many activities other than football: creating fanciful hairstyles, sourcing Mock Tudor accommodation, group sex, modelling, wearing shirts with unfeasibly large collars, lying and cheating, snooker, golf, PlayStation, the covert use of video equipment, text sex, shopping on the Kings Road, chasing foreigners down alleys, spitting with accuracy, spitting with volume, spitting from their noses, lining their pockets, recording pop singles, bringing back the mullet, Jordan, gambling, human ten-pin bowling on days of world mourning, quaffing lager tops, and finding a 'former lapdancer' in a nightclub within 30 seconds.

There are, mind you, a few things with which footballers have not yet proved quite so comfortable: arriving as scheduled to deposit urine, monogamy, foreign languages, basic human decorum, modesty, sensible clothing, abstinence, ambassadorial behaviour when abroad, righting social injustice, singing in tune and handily enough for our purposes . . . talking.

Most of them, advisably, keep it simple. 'The lad's done ever so well and I've just caught it on my left peg and, luckily enough, it's gone in.' There are no prizes for this lot. However, there are others who can't curb their natural sense of adventure and want to try something a little different, fancy themselves to expand a little, maybe even address the question. Admirable sentiments indeed, though, sadly, it's usually just what leads them to come unstuck . . . and move into contention for the Gaffta.

ALSO-RANS

☆Carlton Palmer

In a nutshell: Second-touch-a-tackle England player who kicked off the decline of international football.
Gaffta Panel Verdict: Hard as he tries, Carlton's gaffes aren't nearly as bad as his passing.

On the crisis at Wimbledon:
'Dennis Wise, Vinnie Jones and John Fashanu must be turning in their graves.'

'Unless the chairman decides to sack me, I won't be quitting.'

'I said to the players before the start, "Just go out and give it 100 per cent." I am not asking for any more than that . . .'

☆Frank Worthington

In a nutshell: Dressed like an extra from *Midnight Cowboy* – think Le Tiss and Stringfellow rolled into one.
Gaffta Panel Verdict: Guff style summed up neatly by the title of his autobiography: *One Hump or Two*.

'I had 11 clubs – 12 if you count Stringfellow's.'

'Where did I first meet my wife? I suppose I first met her on Page Three, actually. I opened the paper and there she was.'

☆John Salako

In a nutshell: Cheery former England international spinning occasional African football punditry gigs out of Nigerian background.

Gaffta Panel Verdict: Does punditry much in the same way as he plays – you don't know what's coming next.

'**The Nigerians are in real trouble now. They're going to have to get their finger out, but it is not going to be easy as their backs are against the wall.**'

On the same Nigerians:
'**A lot of chiefs in there and not enough Indians.**'

'**Sportsmanship goes on everywhere, and it is rife in Africa. It's all about trying to unsettle opponents.**'

☆Michael Owen

In a nutshell: Guff's boy-wonder.

Gaffta Panel Verdict: Surprise Gaffta candidate in Alan Shearer mould.

'**I was really surprised when the FA knocked on my doorbell.**'

'**It's great to get the first trophy under the bag.**'

On John Terry:
'**Mentally, he's as strong as an ox.**'

And at last a decent excuse for England not winning things:
'**These tournaments only come along every two years, so you can't expect to win them every year.**'

☆Manu Petit
In a nutshell: Part footballer, part philosopher. Perennial malcontent.
Gaffta Panel Verdict: The sensitive side of guff.

'I'd like to be a dog. Dogs are nice. They can sleep any time, they wag their tails and on top of that they can get stroked all the time.'

'I like the comfort of jeans, and the elegance of a suit. But above all, I love the sensuality and sexuality that emanates from leather. It multiplies one's sensations tenfold.'

☆Gary Neville
In a nutshell: England and United's footballing shop steward.
Gaffta Panel Verdict: Stick to the union meetings, Gary.

'The reason we went out of Euro 2000 wasn't anything to do with what happened in the last minute against Romania.'

'That was extremely disappointing and there can't be any excuses. Chances seemed to go into the goalkeeper's hands, freak goals went against us and the referee was a bit petty.'

NOMINEES

☆David Beckham
In a nutshell: The most famous guff merchant in the world.
Gaffta Panel Verdict: You think these are funny? You should see his penalties.

From one-trick pony wide man to text-addled international sex symbol in ten easy guff steps.

1. Always remember your roots:
'My parents have always been there for me, ever since I was about seven.'

2. Look for the good in everyone:
'Alex Ferguson is the best manager I've ever had at this level. Well, he's the only manager I've actually had at this level. But he's the best manager I've ever had.'

3. Don't neglect your education:
Interviewer: Are you a volatile player?
Becks: Well, I can play in the centre, on the right and occasionally on the left side.

4. Especially the maths:
Guilliem Balague: At least you're still two points clear of Valencia. (After drawing with them at the weekend.)
Becks: I thought it was three after we got a point tonight.

5. Never be afraid of a little experimentation:
'My biggest fashion mistake was probably a pair of ballet shoes I wore as a page boy.'

6. Always keep your options open:
'We've been asked to do *Playboy* together, me and Victoria, as a pair. I don't think I'll ever go naked, but I'll never say never.'

7. Know your mind:
'The thought of pulling on any shirt other than the red one of United just doesn't appeal to me. There's no bigger club in the world than United, so why should I want to leave? I want to stay at Manchester United, become captain and be the best player in the world.'

8. Set clear targets:
'No matter who we're playing against, or who our opponents are, we want to win the game.'

9. There's no time like the present:
'That was in the past – we're in the future now.'

10. Stay spiritual:
'We're definitely going to get Brooklyn christened, but we don't know into which religion!'

☆Paul Merson

In a nutshell: The most miserable guffster around.
Gaffta Panel Verdict: Guff addict.

Poor old Merse is probably the most miserable footballer of our time. And through all of his many personal travails, there was one addiction that gripped more powerfully than the others. It was, of course, his addiction to talking about his addictions. Painful for the 'Magic Man'. Painfully funny for the rest of us.

'I've heard all kinds of wild stories about me, including one in which I was supposed to have been caught half-naked with a bird in the executive box at Highbury. That is complete and utter nonsense. But so many people have asked me about it, I've even wondered at times if it could be true.'

It's probably worth a fiver each way.

'Chairman Peter Hill-Wood spoke out in my favour. I was heartened when he said: "The boy is a mess, his career is in danger. But Arsenal are not going to throw the book at him. He does not have a particularly high intelligence and is unable to cope with the fame and fortune football has brought him."'

With friends like Pete . . .

'I used dope quite a bit when I hung around with my mates, but afterwards I'd always feel very hungry and

have to go to the 24-hour service station and get some Turkish Delight.'

The slippery slope.

'On our wedding night, I was glued to the TV. I sat riveted at the end of the bed on the first night of our honeymoon, watching my 700 quid disappear as Costa Rica beat Scotland.'

Suppose it's Mrs Merse we should feel sorry for, but Scotland, Merse? Come on! Have you not being paying attention at all during your football career?

'If you go to the hairdressers every day, by the seventh day you're going to get a haircut.'

This was Merse suggesting it was time to get out of Middlesbrough before somebody force-fed him the *Racing Post*.

Lately at Walsall, Merse the gaffer has revealed yet another addiction. He's become a workaholic:
'Sometimes, I'm still in work at three in the afternoon.'

If only he still had John Gregory to sort things out:
'The gaffer has given us unbelievable belief.'

☆Eric Cantona
In a nutshell: Collars up. Chest out. Tongue in cheek.
Gaffta Panel Verdict: The Glenn Medeiros of guff. Something of a one-hit wonder.

Eric was the Ronnie Radford of the guff game.

Some players must toil for years before making a name for themselves, but one crisp 40-yard strike, a celebration that unveiled the midriff long before Britney was even born and a soundtrack featuring a young Motty at his most frantic were enough to lift the Hereford journeyman into football folklore.

Seasoned Gaffta veterans like Motson, Robson or Ron may have had to give us a lifetime of gibberish before passing into the Hall of Guff, but Cantona, like Ronnie, made his mark with one devastating utterance of ground-breaking nonsense.

Ronnie's big moment came after he surged through the Edgar Road mud with half of Newcastle in his wake. Eric's, on the other hand, followed a delightful one–two: first a boot up Richard Shaw's backside, and then – as he was trooping off to an early bath – a playful two-footed lunge into the chest of Crystal Palace fan Matthew Simmons, who may have been gently teasing Cantona about his misfortune.

After a kindly beak reduced his original porridge stretch to a few hours playing football with youngsters, Cantona showed up alongside his gaffer and sundry Manchester United bigwigs at a press conference where he was expected to speak of his contrition.

The suits went first with their pleas for redemption. And then someone passed the mic to Eric. The watching media throng was eager. He'd been known to produce some enigmatic moments in the past. 'Idiot, idiot, idiot,' was his Wildean dismissal of three French FA delegates at a disciplinary hearing called when he threw the ball at a referee when playing for Nîmes. He'd later produce an equally eloquent rebuttal of a posse of French journos: 'Look at these small fry. I could piss on them.'

Not a man likely to kowtow before authority then, so the odds were more in favour of rebellion than tears of sorrow. What followed took everyone by surprise, however. Cantona spoke slowly, emphasising each morsel of sagacity for maximum import.

'When the seagulls . . . follow the trawler . . . it's because they think . . . sardines . . . will be thrown . . . into the sea.'
With that, he rose and was gone, before anyone could as much as ask him if this meant a loan spell at Brighton & Hove Albion was on the cards.

For years afterwards, the chattering intelligentsia who

happened to be clambering aboard the football bandwagon at the time racked their brains wondering what the stiff-collared Frenchman could have meant? Was it a withering dismissal of modern media culture and its feeding frenzy? Was he quoting a little-known French philosopher? Did he have any other answers to modern life's vexing demands? Could he be the risen Christ?

Sadly, just as Eric the player was rather often found out on the more taxing European occasions, years later a rounder, hairier Cantona blew the whistle on Eric the philosopher.

'My lawyer and the officials wanted me to speak. So I just said that. It was nothing, it did not mean anything. I could have said, "The curtains are pink but I love them."'

Rimbaud did not yet have an heir then, but, never mind, Cantona's place in the annals of nonsense had been secured.

When he eventually began playing again, Eric scored plenty more goals, picked up a few more red cards and collected a trophy or two. But he would never produce another piece of guff like it. In the end, it may have been the knowledge that he had nothing left to achieve that led to his retirement.

'Leaving a club is like leaving a woman. When you have nothing left to say, you go.'

He'd said enough.

☆Alan Shearer

In a nutshell: The sober face of guff.
Gaffta Panel Verdict: Now that Al is setting out on a media career, perhaps he can let himself go and fulfil his true potential. A contender for the 2008 pundit award?

Who would have thunk it? Alan Shearer popping up alongside Gazza and Wrighty in a list of jokers. The man who's perfected 101 different ways of telling you nothing. 'Mary F***ing Poppins.' The curator, janitor and caretaker of English football's house of clichés.

'It's come down, I've took it on my chest, and thought, if

you don't buy a ticket you don't win the raffle.'

That's the Alan Shearer you thought you knew, playing a straight bat after he banged in two wonder goals on his Blackburn debut. Or the Alan Shearer that was asked how he'd celebrate Rovers' Premiership title win:

'. . . by creosoting the garden fence.'

And yet, while Shearer's may be an entirely accidental brand of humour, just like the mis-kick that flies in off a full-back's arse, they all count. And Big Al has produced more than his fair share of magic moments.

Like the time he gave Richard Keys the full benefit of his medical experience:

Keys: Medial knee ligament damage. Is that serious, Alan?

Shearer: I don't know, Richard. It depends whether it's serious or not.

Or when he was full of praise for Manchester City's new signing:

'Paulo Wanchope is totally unpredictable, but you know what you're going to get when you buy him.'

Of course, the one thing you can say about Shearer is that, on the pitch at least, he wears his heart on his sleeve. Although you wonder whether he'd be quite so committed if he knew he could buy a similar sleeve down the local sports shop:

'No money in the world can buy a white England shirt.'

Alan knows, however, that you've got to make the most of every chance you're given. As he said himself:

'You only get one opportunity of an England debut.'

Whatever glory and riches come his way, though, Shearer is modest to the end:

'One accusation you can't throw at me is that I've always done my best.'

As a Geordie boy, naturally Newcastle is Alan's big love. And he plans to hang around there for quite some time: **'I've never wanted to leave. I'm here for the rest of my life, and hopefully after that as well.'**

Perhaps he should check with Glenn Hoddle whether he's done enough to get a contract next time round. And while he's at it, perhaps Glenn – or Eileen Drewery maybe – might confirm Alan's verdict on some of his old England teammates: **'There's no way the future's over for Martin Keown, Tony Adams or David Seaman.'**

Famously, Alan doesn't like Manchester United and, after he twice opted not to sign for them, Manchester United doesn't like him, their fans regularly suggesting in song that Al 'stinks of piss'. Like everything else, Alan takes this rivalry very seriously. Unfortunately – although perhaps understandably given that he once escaped punishment for attempting to decapitate Neil Lennon – he seems a little unclear on the laws of the game governing random violence: **'At times they don't like you to kick them and they feel you're not allowed to kick them.'**
Shearer's no fool, though. When it comes to the rulebook, he knows the laws that count: **'Football's not just about scoring goals – it's about winning.'**
Now that's the Shearer we know and love.

☆Maradona
In a nutshell: Hand of God. Mouth of Jack Duckworth.
Gaffta Panel Verdict: Becks obsession aside, just misses out on big prize.

Rotund football/volleyball genius Diego Armando Maradona was once described by none other than Bob Wilson as 'a flawed genius who became a genius who is flawed'. That nicely sums him up, because the Maradona of today is pretty much the same wayward, eccentric loose cannon of yesteryear, except without the football talent. It was sad to witness him in a recent documentary struggling to make an impression in a game of three-a-side on a tennis court with his mates. Sadder still was to see him at a Cuban health farm getting hosed down with cold water by a nameless, scantily clad blonde. (Presumably one of the staff.) With the health and other issues he's dealing with nowadays, it's hard to believe that as recently as 1994, he was playing in the World Cup finals.

For the Diego of today, it's all about TV. That's his new cash cow. And what bigger TV audience than the US of A. Better butter them up then . . .

'It was very emotional to watch how well the Americans played, with such heart.'

It's a different story with the old foes, England. He'll not let that one lie:

'I would do it again.'

'It was like pick-pocketing the English and stealing a win.'

No regrets, then, for that infamous case of divine intervention in the 1986 World Cup semi-final. It was such a big occasion that, to Diego, it was almost like . . . international football:

'It was as if we had beaten a country, more than just a football team.'

He looked forward to history repeating itself in 2002:

'The English are absolutely terrified of us. They are quaking in their boots.'

Rather more outrageously . . .

'Argentina is the only serious team of all those playing in the tournament.'

It's all because he loves his country so much:
'When I wear the national team shirt, its sole contact with my skin makes it stand on end.'
His skin stands on end, or the shirt stands on end? Both unlikely propositions.

But it all went wrong for Argentina. He consoled himself by anticipating great things from Juan Sebastian Veron, despite the growing body of evidence that that this faith might be misplaced:
'I identify myself most with "The Witch".'

But there's one Englishman Diego seems to quite like . . . Beckham, of course:
'He's so handsome . . . he looks like a woman.'

Aghast at the reaction these remarks elicited, he felt it necessary to defend himself:
'If I say Beckham is a pretty boy, suddenly they say I'm gay or that Beckham's gay. It's not like that. Nobody's gay.'

A case of protesting too much? There are some dubious actions he's certainly not up for:
'Getting the ball outside the area and not being efficient is like dancing with your sister.'

He's nothing if not a religious man:
'God makes me play well. That is why I always make the sign of the cross when I walk out onto the field. I feel I would be betraying Him if I didn't.'

Fair enough, but it seems that in the manner of a Pharaoh, he wants to take his minions to the afterlife with him:
'I saw death close up and I wanted [the fans holding a vigil outside the hospital] to cover me, to caress me. When God decides it's time, I guess He'll come for us.'

But not everyone is Diego's friend. Pelé, miffed that he had to share the Footballer of the Century award with Diego, questioned whether Diego had 'sufficient greatness as a person' to deserve it. Diego was in no doubt as to who really deserved it, though:

'I had the vote of the people. Pelé won by the book.'

The People's Champion – that's Maradona.

WINNER

☆Paul 'Gazza' Gascoigne

In a nutshell: From mazy dribbler to dribbling idiot.

Gaffta Panel Verdict: You'd get as much sense out of the Gateshead Five – as *The Sun* labelled pal Jimmy's set of bellies when launching a campaign to free Jimmy from the nick.

Poor old Gazza – from the north of London to the north of China, his was a varied and turbulent football career. Some of the highlights include:

- subjecting his 'minder' Jimmy Five Bellies to torture for money
- belching into Italian microphones
- releasing rubbish (and yet strangely chart-topping) singles with Lindisfarne
- blubbing during the World Cup semi-final
- wearing fake breasts in airports
- fishing for koi carp in Chinese hotel ponds
- miming the words 'f***ing w***er' on a family TV programme
- losing at table tennis to Tim Lovejoy on Soccer AM in a storm of foul language.

In latter days, he's had what looks to have been a one-off stint as an incomprehensible pundit for ITV during the 2002 World Cup. And now he's managed to sneak on to the lower rungs of the managerial ladder, where he can put into practice his approach to minimising the effect of suspensions by simply omitting the suspended players from his team selections:

'Because of the booking, I will miss the Holland game – if selected.'

Genius.

Some consider Gazza to be a class clown by nature, others a village idiot. But all agree that he is not exactly an intellectual. Bobby Robson famously said that Gazza was 'daft as a brush'. Gazza was quick with a rebuttal:

'I'm daft, but I wouldn't say I'm daft as a *brush*.'

No, a brush is to all intents and purposes 100 per cent daft, whereas Gazza is probably a few per cent short of perfection in the daftness stakes. But his mathematical abilities, while not quite the finished product, are tantalisingly close to being up to the job . . .

'I've had fourteen bookings this season – eight of which were my fault, but seven of which were disputable.'

So near and yet so far.

As a footballer, Gazza knows it's important to look after himself, especially when coming back from injury:

'The cast [for a broken arm] was due off in hospital any day and I was a bit bored so I decided to cut it off in the kitchen and spiked myself.'

His is a very strict health regimen:

'I've given up beer and guzzling. My only lapse is to have a few toffees.'

Of course, you never know what's around the corner:

'I never predict anything, and I never will.'

And you've got to keep your quality standards high. This was Gazza's prime concern when in the recording studio with Lindisfarne:

'The record's going quite well. I didn't want it released if it sounded like shit. If it were sounding shit, people might think "that sounds like shit" and that wouldn't be much good, like.'

But Gazza's nothing if not a great communicator. Above all, he listens. That's why ITV sent him out to talk to the general public.

Gazza: Did you watch the match?
Worker on building site: Yeah.
Gazza: Did you watch it?
Worker: Yeah, the boss gave us time off.
Gazza: Does your boss know you watched it?

He wasn't happy at all when George Best started slagging him off in the tabloids, but he soon shut Bestie up with put-downs such as this:

'The fat man . . . he's absolutely slaughtered us just for a bit of cash, and that's a scum bastard.'

It is indeed, Gazza. It is indeed.

THE 'GET AN ATLAS' AWARD

THE GAFFTA AWARDS

10. 'Costacurta, the Portuguese international . . . Shevchenko, the Uruguayan international . . .'
Trevor Welch

9. 'Newport 0, Wrexham 1. Well done to the Welsh there.'
Radio 2 newsreader

8. 'Romania are more Portuguese than German.'
Barry Venison

7. 'The Belgians will play like their fellow Scandinavians, Denmark and Sweden.'
Andy Townsend

6. 'Chesterfield 1, Chester 1. Another score draw in the local derby.'
Des Lynam

5. 'Ajax have players from all over the world, from Africa, Egypt, Belgium.'
Noel King

4. 'They've given themselves a mountain . . . er . . . Mount Everest . . . which is just around the corner from here.'
John Aldridge was in Basel, Switzerland

3. 'It's only a small place, Deportivo.'
Mark Lawrenson

2. 'It was like living in a different country.'
Ian Rush on his time at Juventus

1. 'I'd like to play for an Italian club, like Barcelona.'
Mark Draper

BEST ANCHOR AWARD

An anchor, in the sailing sense, is essentially a huge lump of deadweight that scrapes along the bottom until it snags some bit of detritus or rubbish. Funnily enough, a TV anchor is often not very much different. What was Des Lynam on ITV if not a deadweight? What does Gary Lineker do in the BBC studio except scrape along until he snags some quip that exploits the lowest common denominator?

All right, that's a bit harsh. Lynam and Lineker are generally streets ahead of the degenerates and spoofers they have to work with – the so-called 'analysts'. And lest we forget, the peerless Jeff Stelling proudly flies the flag of dignified anchor-hood week in, week out.

But it's not like it used to be. Gone are the days when Jimmy Hill and Brian Moore would steer *Match of the Day* and *The Big Match*, respectively, around the metaphorical rocks and sandbanks of low budgets and primitive technology, running the whole show like Mississippi riverboat pilots of old, except strangely bemused and befuddled ones. Nowadays, it's all ultra-slick and comparatively soulless. Especially Richard Keys over on Sky, who is the anchor equivalent of an SAS operative. For him, verbal lapses are few and swiftly passed over. It drains the coverage of life – it conveys torpor, tedium and jadedness, rather than excitement.

Nevertheless, the fact remains that when it's your job to talk to camera on live TV without an autocue (or in the case of Irish TV3's Trevor Welch, even with an autocue), there is the potential for all manner of verbal calamity.

Perhaps it's fitting that the Gaffta Awards is the only awards ceremony around that's not 'anchored' by somebody. Long may this anchorless tradition continue . . .

THE ALSO-RANS

☆Garth Crooks

In a nutshell: Pseudo-intellectual, pompous, tiresome . . . and occasionally hilarious.

Gaffta Panel Verdict: In spite of modest nonsense output, an important figure in the guff game, if only for. The way. He speaks. In halting. Sentences. To give a. False sense of. Import. To the usual old. Rubbish. He's spouting.

'Football's football. If that weren't the case it wouldn't be the game that it is.'

'You've got to get that spot on or you look foolish and he did.'

'Sven, I can confirm that England have qualified for the last 16.'

Cheers, Garth.

☆Bill O'Herlihy

In a nutshell: Unflappable Irish anchor more than a match for high-powered punditry panel.

Gaffta Panel Verdict: Produces guff, and also selflessly acts as comic foil for TV guests.

'If you don't want to know the scores in the other games tonight, look away now. [Caption shows Pool lead 1–0] Actually, it's one-all now in the Liverpool game.'

'I don't know why they're not playing Nuno Gomes, after all he scored four goals in their match against Andorra, including one hat-trick!'

'Liverpool v. Middlesbrough. This one was an early afternoon kick-off for both sides.'

'I'm contemplating Totti, in a sense.'

☆Gabby Logan

In a nutshell: The only lady to brave the guff men's club.

Gaffta Panel Verdict: Won't be pleased to miss out on nomination. We could see a bout of handbags.

'Robbie and I have been sweating there all week and we weren't really doing anything.'

'Fourteen million of you were watching that game on ITV, that's 87 per cent of the population.'

☆Bob Wilson

In a nutshell: Pre-Premiership *Football Focus* anchor – solid citizen.

Gaffta Panel Verdict: Out of the broadcasting game too long, living off reputation alone.

'There's one that hasn't been cancelled because of the

Arctic conditions – it's been cancelled because of a frozen pitch.'

'Spurs, one of the in-form teams of the moment with successive wins, are almost as impressive as Queens Park Rangers with five.'

'Liverpool have now really got to win two away – one in Barcelona, the other at home to Roma.'

☆Ian Payne
In a nutshell: Former Beeb radio man now working in the shadow of Keys.
Gaffta Panel Verdict: An up-and-comer. Increased air time = greater guff/gaffe potential.

'Tomorrow, the whole of Newcastle v. Manchester United.'

'The Laudrup brothers can turn on a herring.'

'Aston Villa are seventh in the League – that's almost as high as you can get without being one of the top six.'

☆Elton Welsby
In a nutshell: Face of north-western football coverage and pre-Des ITV anchor who has slipped into radio obscurity.
Gaffta Panel Verdict: Regional anchor made good – always seemed to be on borrowed time as ITV's main man.

'And now the goals from Carrow Road, where the game finished 0–0.'

'Football today would certainly not be the same if it had not existed.'

☆Ray Stubbs

In a nutshell: Sack of potatoes on *Football Focus* sofa.
Gaffta Panel Verdict: Lame verbal sparring with Lawro a major minus.

'You can't do more than score three goals away from home.'

'In the bottom nine positions of the league, there are nine teams.'

'Cometh the hour, cometh the moment.'

And on Gazza in China:
'He keeps calling everybody over there by the same name: "Way Hay Man".'

THE NOMINEES

☆Jimmy Hill

In a nutshell: Grand old chin of English football.
Gaffta Panel Verdict: Cannot quite recapture his guff heyday over croissants and orange juice.

Forget 1966. It was 1999 when we really thought it was all over. No not the baby-faced assassin's jammy Nou Camp winner – worse than that. For '99 was the year when world football's most famous chin would cast its last and longest shadow into our living rooms. Yes, Jimmy Hill retired. And those of us left behind would have to look elsewhere for guidance. We would scramble in the dust – Big Ron's gold dust maybe – for a new moral compass.

Or so we thought. As the beautiful game lurched from scandal to crisis in his absence, Jimmy could stand for it no more. He would find a way to bring back reason and, what's more, he'd do it without leaving the house. And so Jimmy Hill's *Sunday Supplement* was born. Nowadays, Jimmy addresses his flock every Sunday morning from the comfort of his kitchen. Not only that, each week he invites three of Fleet Street's oiliest scribes into his home to be cleansed. And to think some folk still look elsewhere to explain declining church attendance.

It means, however, that Jimmy's favoured guff technique has evolved somewhat. In the old days, he'd perfected a flawless good cop, bad cop guff-fest with El Tel. Nowadays, however, you're more likely to encounter the rather scarier prospect of Jim leaving the breakfast table to 'pop out and baste my meat'.

THE HILL GUFFBANK:

'England now have three fresh men, with three fresh legs.'

'We're not used to weather in June in this country.'

'It wasn't a bad performance, but you can't tell whether it was good or bad.'

'In the words of the old song, it's a long time from May to December, but, you know, it's an equally long time from December to May.'

'Beckham has two feet, which a lot of players don't have nowadays.'

'Even if you tap it in from one yard, it counts in the record books as a goal, unlike the chances you miss.'

'If England are going to win this match, they're going to have to score a goal.'

'It is a cup final and the one who wins it goes through.'

'We have one David Beckham playing abroad and if Owen goes, that would be two.'

☆ Gary Lineker
In a nutshell: The Princess Di of football coverage.
Gaffta Panel Verdict: Signed off with a crap game in Sweden. Now signs off with crap gags on the Beeb.

Former Spurs and England (and current Walker's Crisps) star Gary Lineker had a rocky time during his transition from striker to anchor. Annoying and stilted at the beginning on *Match of the Day*, he struggled, despite years of service for his national side, to win over the viewers. He found his stride eventually, though, and became something of a master of the one-liner. Maybe lately he's become a bit too comfortable in front of the camera, tending to lapse into self-indulgence. That might be understandable with the likes of Alan Hansen and Peter Reid in the studio. If he doesn't indulge himself, who else is going to do it? In any case, it doesn't take too much in the way of self or any other kind of indulgence for Lineker to stick his foot into his mouth:

'Someone has to save the club from existence.'
Leicester really need to be put out of their misery.

'The Polish coach said if they win the World Cup, he'll shave his head off.'
Drastic measures indeed.

'Ronaldo: the man who could eat an apple through a tennis racket.'
Schoolyard stuff.

'The World Cup is every four years, so it's going to be a perennial problem.'
Dictionary for Mr Lineker.

'There's no in-between – you're either good or bad. We were in-between.'
No in-between here. Just plain bad.

'For Premiership clubs, Peter, these are no-win games. Unless you win.'
It seems obvious, but . . .

'Football is where 22 players run round after the ball and at the end the Germans always win.'
Rueful Lineker tells it like it is.

'It's a case of him [Eric Cantona] losing *les marbles*.'
A bon mot.

'An excellent player, Ian Wright. But he does have a black side.'
What gave it away?

'This game is what my children would describe as "pants".'
Street-talkin' Lineker's down with the kids.

'To be honest, it would have been better to watch it on Ceefax.'
Lineker lambastes Wimbledon.

'The BBC aren't interested in buying Wimbledon, but maybe Ceefax would be?'
Elephant-memory Lineker follows up his own joke years later.

'Before the tournament, Pelé was telling me how he liked Butt. Bet he prefers Rs. All three of them.'

Lineker drags Ronaldo, Ronaldinho and Rivaldo down with him.

☆Richard Keys

In a nutshell: Football's hairiest PR man.

Gaffta Panel Verdict: Difficult to incorporate guff into a sales pitch.

A man with the public relations skills of Max Clifford, Alistair Campbell and Goebbels rolled into one. If your name's Rupert and you're looking to drum up interest in coverage of a humdrum football competition, Richard Keys is your man.

When it comes to hype, Keys is the finished article. Plucked from the wasteland of breakfast television in 1992, his incredibly hairy hands are all over the success of *The Premiership*. Single-handedly responsible for introducing the dubious phrase 'The Greatest League in the World' into civilised society, Keys also charges and replaces Andy Gray's batteries before every broadcast, revving the Scot into a frenzy about the prospect of Bolton grabbing a 'massive, massive' three points at home to Everton.

Of course, so smooth a broadcaster is Keys, he doesn't actually make any gaffes – that is, if you exclude the pastel sports jackets he made his signature during his early outings.

However, when you've developed an interview style that must avoid any criticism of the sometimes wretched product you're hawking, the prospect of some notably bland conversations is inevitable. To many, it is these information-free exchanges that have become Keys' guff trademark.

Bigging up another Man Utd v. Arsenal 'title decider', Keys really put Alan Smith on the spot:

Keys: What wins championships, forwards or defenders?
Smudger: [sheepishly] Well, it's a bit of both really, isn't it?

As Liverpool gaffer Roy Evans began one of his final seasons, Keys famously extracted every last ounce of insight:

Keys: Well, Roy, do you think you'll have to finish above Man United to win the league?
Roy Evans: You have to finish above everyone to win the league, Richard.

As kick-off loomed in one of Sky's self-styled 'dates with destiny', Keys braced himself and his colleagues for the fray.

Keys: Alan Smith, are you ready?
Alan Smith: Yes.
Keys: Gary Pallister, are you ready?
Gary Pallister: [wriggling] Yes.

The Keys line of questioning also seems to bring out the best in his interviewees.

Wondering if Gary Speed was close to returning from injury:

Keys: Are you far away, Gary?
Speed: No. About 20 minutes down the road.

Probing Trevor Francis's managerial techniques:

Francis: I once got a sports psychologist involved during my time with Birmingham.
Keys: And what exactly did he do, Trevor?
Francis: Well, it's a mental thing really.

Very occasionally, Keys manages some genuine guff all on his own. As a camera lovingly closed in on David Ginola, tenderly doing his stretches and caressing his hands through his flowing locks, he produced one of his finest hours:

'There's Ginola. He's one of Everton's tools today.'

And then there was recovering triple-addict Paul Merson's famous outing in the Sky studio. Concerned at some profligate Arsenal finishing, sensitive Keysy cut to the chase:

'You'd have put your house on Ian Wright scoring that one.'
Heartless.

☆ Des Lynam

In a nutshell: The only man who could possibly make guff sexy.
Gaffta Panel Verdict: No ladies on the Gaffta panel, so Des just misses out.

One of the most controversial and talked about transfers in the history of the British game was the move of housewife's choice Des Lynam from the BBC to ITV. Suave, witty, urbane – Lynam was the quintessential Englishman (albeit an Irish one), the essence of the BBC. In fact, for a time when Des was at the very height of his powers, he more or less was the BBC – popping up to guest host not just every sports programme that caught his fancy but also episodes of *Holiday* and many more besides.

In fact, it was the increasing reliance of Auntie on Lynam's broad shoulders that played a part in him deciding to leave the network. On the eve of his decision to go, the Beeb had planned to install Lynam as its main news anchor, as well as host of the *Antiques Roadshow*, *The Generation Game* and that contest that Wrighty marshals between the boys and the girls.

Apparently, Des felt that he was moving away from his true love – sport, and football primarily – and he quit to go over to the other side, like Morecambe and Wise before him, to anchor ITV's coverage of the Premiership and the Champions League.

Sadly his star then faded somewhat – he cut an

increasingly dejected figure as he marked time to see out his ITV contract. No wonder: where once he had worked with Hansen and Lawrenson, he was now confronted by the likes of McCoist and Earle. To further add to his misery, he developed a more pronounced squint in the nuclear glare of the ITV studios. And if these things weren't bad enough, he found his phlegmatic approach undermined by ITV's lust for advertising revenue – allowing him precious little time to kick back and relax as he once did on the Beeb.

Hemmed in by the grubby world of money-making and pandering to the lowest common denominator, Des found it increasingly difficult to remain dignified.

Eventually, he effected an escape from ITV's clutches, securing a new BBC contract. But Lineker now holds sway on *Match of the Day* and Rory Bremner has become better at being Des than the man himself. Now he's back on home ground, can Des regain the title of the most convincing Des Lynam in broadcasting?

THE LYNAM GUFFBANK:

'More football later, but first let's see the goals from the Scottish Cup final.'

'Kicked wide of the goal with such precision.'

'Peter Shilton conceded five, you don't get many of those to the dozen.'

'Poborsky's had one or two moments – two, actually.'

'Arsenal could have got away with a 0–0 if it wasn't for the two goals.'

'He was unlucky, or was it just bad luck?'

**Terry Venables: It's either a penalty or it's not a penalty.
Des Lynam: Sometimes it can be neither.**

'Chesterfield 1, Chester 1 – another score draw in the local derby.'

'It's a renaissance, or, put more simply, some you win, some you lose.'

'We did this [built up England's chances] at the last World Cup and then all of a sudden . . . bonk.'

WINNER

☆Jeff Stelling

In a nutshell: The Sky *Soccer Saturday* zookeeper.
Gaffta Panel Verdict: Achieves the impossible. Remains a suave, dignified figure even when up to his knees in guff.

Classy Jeff Stelling is surely Hartlepool's most debonair export. A natural for the part of Bond (Diamonds are for Trevor? Never Say Neville Again?) had Pierce Brosnan not so outrageously usurped him, Jeff is a picture of suave dignity each Saturday afternoon in the high-pressure hothouse of the *Gillette Soccer Saturday* studio. Not only does he have to field constant chatter in his earpiece in order to keep a steady stream of football data flowing, but in the midst of this he also has to deal with the tragi-comic shenanigans of the likes of Rod Marsh, Charlie Nicholas and sometimes even George Best.

Unfortunately, sometimes the information Jeff receives in

his earpiece is of questionable use, and in the heat of the moment, his quality-control process can fail. One Saturday, York were playing Yeovil:

'It's the first time that two teams have started a league game where both teams begin with that letter.'

On other occasions, Jeff can't quite blame the researchers:

'That's Steve Howey's third-ever league goal, and he's never scored more than two in a season before.'

'Chris Porter scored his first league goal last week, and he's done the same this week.'

'At Fratton Park, only Manchester United have scored more home goals.'

Sometimes, though, Jeff's information is right on the money, and ever so predictable:

'There's been a penalty awarded at Old Trafford – I don't think you need me to tell you which way it's gone.'

Given the amount of talk ultra-professional Jeff gets through every Saturday, perhaps it's understandable that he occasionally utters what one, regrettably, must characterise as complete nonsense:

'It's end to end stuff, all at one end.'

'Not much doubt about the pen. Although, looking again, it might have been outside the box, but other than that . . . actually, it might have been a dive as well.'

'The gravy train has hit the bucket.'

'One-dimensional Liverpool may be, but what a dimension it is!'

Mostly, honest Jeff calls it like it is, sometimes to his own cost. He might well have blown any chance of a step up to the *Ford Super Sunday* gig with this remark:

'I noticed this week he [Rooney] drives a Ford car. Can you imagine his teammates absolutely murdering him at traffic lights?'

Maybe because of all the practice he gets dealing with the inanities of the jokers around him, Jeff has developed a nice line in corny one-liners. When Kevin Nolan equalised for Bolton against Liverpool, he had this to say:

'His sisters will be proud of him.'

At least once a week, he wheels out this old chestnut:

'Total Network Solutions 1, Caernarfon 0. They'll be dancing in the streets of T.N.S. tonight.'

And here's how he bade the lads adieu for a well-earned week's R&R:

'I'm off next week. I'll miss you guys like Michael Jackson misses Martin Bashir.'

Speaking of the lads, Jeff is a dab hand at putting them in their places:

Stelling: I hear [the Irish squad] spent the week running and watching videos.
Nicholas: What kind of videos?
Stelling: Not the kind you watch, Charlie.

And he's not afraid to threaten extreme sanction against Rod Marsh when his supreme self-control slips:

'Have you heard about the Turkish pundit who was shot five times, Rodney?'

And then, of course, there's the all-time Stelling classic. George Best was an absentee, having famously just had a couple of thousand quid stolen from him by two lovely ladies he had invited back to his hotel room. Stelling's verdict?

'He's not feeling too grand.'

LIFETIME ACHIEVEMENT AWARD: BILL SHANKLY

'**Some people believe football is a matter of life and death. I am very disappointed with that attitude. I can assure you it is much, much more important than that.**'

For this utterance alone, Bill Shankly was the name on many people's lips when the Gaffta Board proposed setting up a Hall of Fame to honour the high kings of guff. It's a much-repeated piece of nonsense that captures the madness of the football fanatic like no other. It is but one example of the genius that was Bill Shankly, the single most brilliant football-speak merchant in the history of the game. Some say there was no football guff before Shankly.

Put it this way, if there was a Guffsters' Guffster of the Year, Shanks would've had a mantelpiece full of them. In fact, they'd fight toe-to-toe with his Guff Writers' Guffster of the Year Awards for space above the fire.

Shankly was a colossus who bestrode the world of football-speak: a humorist, socialist and populist legend of the game, he is unsurpassed in his brilliance, despite his pomp having been in the pre-blanket-TV-coverage era. If he were alive today, he'd be the most sought-after and highest-paid media pundit of them all. Marsh, McClintock and Mullery would be dwarfed by his presence on *Gillette Soccer Saturday*. Allen, Spackman and Cottee would scurry for cover. Stelling would have a panellist of equal substance to himself.

Shankly's body of work has both depth and breadth. In fact, it's staggering, given that the media of his time didn't have the insatiable appetite for soundbites that is so widespread today. One can only imagine how he'd revel in post-match interviews with Keys and Gray. Five hours on a Saturday with Stelling would've been a mouthwatering prospect. Liverpool FC's website would've become the virtual equivalent of the Tannoy he used as Carlisle manager to discuss his team selection with the fans. One slavers when one thinks of what might have been. Bill Shankly was a man before his time.

And just how many more anecdotes of the man would have come to light? For this was a man who once arrived in the Liverpool dressing-room in a dishevelled state only 20 minutes before kick-off having been out on the Kop to be with the fans. He was the man who insisted that Liverpool travel on a Friday afternoon to away games so that he could arrive in the evening in time to see *The Untouchables*. He was the man who reputedly was discovered shouting at a light bulb in an Eastern European hotel, berating the spies of the home side! He was a man and manager apart.

Shanks' guff was philosophical, visionary, humorous, populist, cutting but never malicious or wilfully hurtful. Well, not unless you were an Everton fan. Much of it is downright legendary – standing the test of time as if cut in stone.

THE LEGENDARY:

'If you are first, you are first. If you are second, you are nothing.'

'Just go out and drop a few hand grenades all over the place, son.'
Advice to a young Kevin Keegan.

'Take that poof bandage off. And what do you mean *your* knee. It's *Liverpool's* knee!'
Admonishment for Tommy Smith after he turned up for training with a bandaged knee.

'You, son, could start a riot in a graveyard.'
Again, to Tommy Smith.

'I told this player: "Listen, son, you haven't broken your leg. It's all in the mind."'

'Of course I didn't take my wife to see Rochdale as an anniversary present. It was her birthday. Would I have got married in the football season? Anyway, it was Rochdale reserves.'

'With him in defence, we could play Arthur Askey in goal.'
High praise for Ron Yeats.

'If a player is not interfering with play or seeking to gain an advantage, then he should be.'

'It's great grass at Anfield, professional grass.'

'Nonsense! I've kicked every ball, headed out every cross. I once scored a hat-trick. One was lucky, but the others were great goals.'
After being told that he had never experienced playing in a derby.

THE PHILOSOPHICAL:
'My idea was to build Liverpool into a bastion of invincibility. Napoleon had that idea. He wanted to conquer the bloody world. I wanted Liverpool to be untouchable. My idea was to build Liverpool up and up until eventually everyone would have to submit and give in.'

'My life is my work. My work is my life.'

'Football is a simple game based on the giving and taking of passes, of controlling the ball and of making yourself available to receive a pass. It is terribly simple.'

'Above all, I would like to be remembered as a man who was selfless, who strove and worried so that others could share the glory, and who built up a family of people who could hold their heads up high and say, "We're Liverpool."'

'I've been a slave to football. It follows you home, it follows you everywhere, and eats into your family life. But every working man misses out on some things because of his job.'

'Fire in your belly comes from pride and passion in wearing the red shirt. We don't need to motivate players, because each of them is responsible for the performance of the team as a whole. The status of Liverpool's players keeps them motivated.'

'I was the best manager in Britain because I was never devious or cheated anyone. I'd break my wife's legs if I played against her, but I'd never cheat her.'

THE POPULIST:
'I'm a people's man – only the people matter.'

'The fans here are the greatest in the land. They know the game, and they know what they want to see. The people on the Kop make you feel great, yet humble.'

'At a football club, there's a holy trinity – the players, the manager and the supporters. Directors don't come into it. They are only there to sign the cheques.'

'I'm just one of the people who stands on the Kop. They think the same as I do, and I think the same as they do. It's a kind of marriage of people who like each other.'

'Although I'm a Scot, I'd be proud to be called a Scouser.'

'I was only in the game for the love of football – and I wanted to bring back happiness to the people of Liverpool.'

THE HUMOROUS:

'The problem with you, son, is that all your brains are in your head.'

'Sickness would not have kept me away from this one. If I'd been dead, I would have had them bring the casket to the ground, prop it up in the stands and cut a hole in the lid.'

'He has football in his blood,' a disappointed scout complained, speaking of a trialist at Liverpool.
'You may be right,' Shankly said, 'but it hasn't reached his legs yet.'

Shanks: Where are you from?
Fan: I'm a Liverpool fan from London.
Shanks: Well, laddie, what's it like to be in heaven?

'I only wanted him for the reserves.'
To his players after failing to sign Lou Macari in 1973.

Tommy Docherty: A hundred thousand wouldn't buy him.
Shanks: Yeah, I am one of the hundred thousand.

Ray Clemence: Sorry, boss, I should have kept my legs together.
Shanks: Wrong. It's your mother who should have!

'He's worse than the rain in Manchester. At least the rain in Manchester stops occasionally.'
On Brian Clough.

Shanks: When you get the ball, I want you to beat a couple of men and smash the ball into the net, just the same way you used to at Bury.
Lindsay: But, Boss, that wasn't me. It was Bobby Kerr.
Shankly, turning to Bob Paisley: Christ, Bob, we've signed the wrong player.

THE LOCAL RIVALRY:

'If Everton were playing at the bottom of the garden, I'd pull the curtains.'

'I know this is a sad occasion, but I think that Dixie would be amazed to know that even in death he could draw a bigger crowd than Everton can on a Saturday afternoon.'

Barber: Anything off the top?
Shanks: Aye. Everton.

'A lot of football success is in the mind. You must believe you are the best, and then make sure that you are. In my time at Anfield we always said we had the best two teams on Merseyside: Liverpool and Liverpool Reserves.'

'Don't worry, Alan. At least you'll be able to play close to a great team!'
To Alan Ball, who had just signed for Everton.

BEST PUNDIT AWARD

The French call pundits 'consultants'. Since consultants, in the business sense of the word, are by and large people whose job it is to talk nebulously about topics they may or may not understand, only to be remunerated generously for their supposed efforts, the term is a well-chosen one.

Is the English word equally well chosen? Well, take a look in the dictionary and you'll see two definitions of the word 'pundit'. The first says that a pundit is simply a learned individual. This is the original meaning of the word, which comes from the Hindi *pandit*, a 'wise man'. The second definition of pundit is rather more pertinent – it says that the pundit is someone who makes observations in an authoritative manner. That, obviously, is more closely in line with what we observe on our television sets every week. Ally McCoist would not be described by many as a 'wise man'. On the other hand, he does make observations about football matches in an authoritative way. The tragedy is that he seems to have succeeded in fooling most of the people most of the time into thinking that he is in fact 'wise', at least ITV viewers anyhow.

The likes of Alan Hansen might at one time have been credibly regarded as a wise football man. Nowadays, though, he's more of a parody of his old punditry self, and is, again, more of a maker of authoritative-sounding remarks than a dispenser of wisdom.

It's a sad state of affairs. Where, among BBC (Hansen, Wrighty, Schmeichel, Reid), ITV (McCoist, Allen, Earle) or even Sky (have you seen Kenny Sansom in action?), can we find wisdom these days? Arguably, the answer is 'nowhere'. Where have the giants of the punditry game gone? Who were they were in the first place? Indeed, do we really need pundits?

Well, we might not need their opinions, but tear them out of the football tapestry and you have, to mix a metaphor, collapsed the mineshaft leading to one of the very richest seams of guff and nonsense.

THE ALSO-RANS

☆Phil Neal

In a nutshell: Great player. Parroting assistant coach. Crap pundit.

Gaffta Panel Verdict: Needs to copy some of Graham Taylor's guff.

On the problems associated with regularly sacking your manager:
'You end up with Cadbury's Allsorts.'

To Jim Smith:
'You were a hinchpin in midfield.'

On the mysteries of international travel:
'The time in the world has gotten shorter so it doesn't take so long to get to Australia.'

Warning England fans not to travel to Turkey:
'There could be fatalities. Or even worse, injuries.'

☆Charlie Nicholas

In a nutshell: Questionable dress sense . . . even more questionable word sense.

Gaffta Panel Verdict: Has successfully sublimated his formerly dissipative ways into the cause of guff.

On Scotland v. Nigeria:
'Every time they attacked we were memorised by them.'

'It's a bit like Frank, Jeff. The teams are having problems with wind.'

'Quinny looks like he's running the wrong way on a conveyor belt.'

☆Robbie Earle

In a nutshell: A cut-price Trevor Brooking for the ITV market share.

Gaffta Panel Verdict: Guff content of utterances weak; information content equally so.

McCoist: You know I think he's just clipped his own leg and gone over. In fact, he's lucky the referee doesn't book him.
Gabby Logan: Robbie?
Earle: I think he's just gone down over his own leg, and, tell you what, he's lucky the referee doesn't book him.

'If you had a linesman on each side of the pitch in both halves, you'd have nearly four . . .'

'This season is going to run and run, almost till the last day.'

'I wouldn't say lucky. I think they've deserved their luck.'

☆ Ray Wilkins

In a nutshell: Absolutely marvellous. Smashing. Quite exceptional, Richard.

Gaffta Panel Verdict: Like his hair, his guff is thin on the ground, but what there is of it is acceptable.

'Ronaldo is always very close to being onside or offside.'

'Fiorentina start the second half attacking their fans; just the way they like things.'

'The gelling period has just started to knit.'

'It's the same in any walk of life. If you put balls in the box, you cause problems.'

'The team must try to get their ship back on the road.'

☆ Peter Reid

In a nutshell: Dodgy geezer. Dodgy guffster.

Gaffta Panel Verdict: Succeeded in assembling a huge squad at Sunderland; has signally failed to assemble a similarly huge library of guff.

Showing off the lingo:
'Magnifico . . . or whatever they say in Paris.'

Not being racist:
'If Anelka's not active there, I'm not being racist, but I'm a Chinaman.'

The ultimate sacrifice for the team:
'Goes at the defender, cuts his left leg off, cuts his left leg off . . .'

'England fans are in high spirits. I was in Lisbon last night and it was on fire.'

Bloody hell, they didn't even manage that in Charleroi.

☆Clive Allen

In a nutshell: Good player in his day; should now, by rights, be selling insurance.

Gaffta Panel Verdict: Occasional amusing remark fails to compensate for largely tedious screen presence.

On Holland v. Germany:
'Straight away, they literally bombed the German box.'

'The French, as a nation, are flushed with top players.'

'They haven't made many sautées forward.'

'You won't beat David Seaman from that distance.'

Since when?

☆Gary Pallister

In a nutshell: United centre-half from less forgetful times.

Gaffta Panel Verdict: Habit of posing provocatively on *Football Focus* couch with legs akimbo. Distracts from his guff output.

'The pitch has been fairly mashed up by the rugby, and that makes for a level playing field.'

'Chris Sutton loves to feel you against him, loves the physical side and likes to get that hole.'

☆Lee Dixon

In a nutshell: Nice-guy image at odds with cut-throat atmosphere in Sky studio.

Gaffta Panel Verdict: If guff career proves as long as his football career, may eventually build up respectable quotes collection.

Explaining the unusual state of affairs in England's group to Ray Stubbs:
'I think points are going to play a part now.'

'John Hartson is a big lad at the best of times.'

'David Seaman's big enough to hold his hand up and say I've made a mistake . . . and he'll do so again.'

☆Ian Wright

In a nutshell: The shrill, more-ITV-than-ITV-themselves face of BBC punditry.

Gaffta Panel Verdict: Would be in contention for Gaffta if we could tolerate listening to him for five minutes.

'Without being too harsh on David Beckham, he cost us the match.'

'I don't make predictions. I never have done and I never will do.'

'My name is usually the one on the end of people's lips.'

'It took a lot of bottle for Tony [Adams] to own up.'

On a little bit of penalty box argy bargy:
'He's having it off with him. What do you have to do to get a penalty? He's spooning him.'

THE NOMINEES

☆Alan Mullery

In a nutshell: Not cut out for punditry, or even talking. Living proof that winning a World Cup opens a few doors.

Gaffta Panel Verdict: The loan of a dictionary would considerably limit his guff output.

Apparently Alan Mullery is considered to be a very good speaker on the after-dinner circuit. So says his management agency anyway. You wouldn't know it from the way he mangles the Queen's English. Never has a man been in such dire need of a dictionary. HRH would have him in the Tower had he not served his country well on the field of play.

'Well, I've seen some tackles, Jonathan, but that was the ultimatum!'

'Jürgen Klinsmann, who refutes to earn £25,000 a week.'

'I can't understand the notoriety of people.'

'He's not going to adhere himself to the fans.'

'It doesn't endow me to be honest.'

'To be fair, I don't think Les Ferdinand was fouled there. He went over on his own ability.'

'We've got to be very careful we don't over-elaborate on the boy's ability.'

Pity Mullers wasn't careful not to over-elaborate here:
'Ipswich's pitch has been voted the best in the Premiership – in terms of surface, that is.'

Even when he's grammatically correct, there's still something not quite right . . .
'When Celtic get an opportunity to go above Rangers, they've got to jump at it with both hands.'

'He has all-round, 365-degree vision.'

'Bridge has done nothing wrong, but his movement's not great and his distribution's been poor.'

Mullers' Shylock-style plea for a modicum of human compassion:
'Roy Evans bleeds red blood.'

And on the subject of blood:
'There's claret all over the place. It's like that Ugandan Beaujolais we had at the Christmas party.'

And finally, it's Mullers, Man of Compassion, dealing with Mark Bosnich's bout of depression:
'Give me the forty grand a week and the pretty girls and I'll be depressed.'

Jeff Stelling tries to eke some trace of understanding out of Mullers about what is, after all, a serious medical condition, but to little avail:
'It is an illness and it's terrible, but if you're sitting in a chair with forty grand a week, you haven't got a problem.'

☆Rodney Marsh

In a nutshell: Likely lad of Sky *Soccer Saturday* set-up.
Gaffta Panel Verdict: Strong contender, but panel feared top prize might go to his head. Obnoxious enough as he is.

Cheeky chappie Rodney Marsh is the workshy '70s midfield stylist turned wide boy of punditry. A wayward maverick who gives five-hour football marathon Sky *Soccer*

Saturday the edge it so keenly needs in order to be watchable. His love–hate relationship with anchor Jeff Stelling produces the programme's finest moments, especially as Rod is unafraid to call a crap game just that, contrary to the strict letter of the Sky ethos. He'd never get away with it if he had to work with Richard Keys, but tolerant Stelling understands the worth of Rod's curmudgeonliness.

Rod: Hunt's come on for Sunderland.
Stelling: You mean Bolton.
Marsh: One of the two.

Rod: Yessss!
Stelling: Rodney?
Rod: It's half-time, Jeff.

Rod's speciality is damnation with faint praise. How about this for a summation of an uninspiring Southampton v. Norwich encounter?
'This game needs a corner.'

Better yet:
'The second half started two minutes late, I reckon the ball refused to come out.'

Sometimes faint praise isn't worth the bother. That's when Rod comes out and just calls a spade a spade:
'I'd rather take Christine Hamilton out to dinner than watch this match.'

This one is just plain mean:
'Campo looks like a fat pub player.'

He's also a dab hand at the bizarre yet apt metaphor:
'Never mind leaping like a salmon, Jeff, he leaps like a goldfish.'

'Derby are like a man with diarrhoea who can't get his trousers off.'

Occasionally, however, it's Rod's powers of communication that go down the toilet:
'We sometimes think of Arsène Wenger as a general media population.'

It's times like this when he must turn to his own fledgling Ronglish-like dialect. Rodglish, anyone?
'Mickey Mouse goalkeeping. A hire-purchase goal. He's gone down in instalments.'

It's not a lingo for the squeamish:
'Wimbledon are putting balls into the blender.'

He's quite keen on a bit of racy fun on the field of play:
'The sub's just pulled his shorts up! You could see all his orchestras! It's fascinating . . . it should be X-rated!'

But he's nothing if not an experienced leader of men:
'All a manager has to do is keep 11 players happy – the 11 in the reserves. The first team are happy because they are in the first team.'

And finally, it's Rod Marsh, working-class hero:
'Most people are in a factory from nine till five. Their job may be to turn out 263 little circles. At the end of the week they're three short and somebody has a go at them. On Saturday afternoons, they deserve something to go and shout about.'

☆Terry Venables
In a nutshell: Another punditry wide boy. Crafty.
Gaffta Panel Verdict: Tel's guff comes from everywhere – doubtless in a Christmas tree formation.

El Tel has been there, done that. Whether belting out a stirring Sinatra number to an audience of drunken footballers, shouting instructions to Gary Kelly from the Elland Road technical area or bestowing the benefit of his wisdom on ITV's Matt Smith, everything Tel does, he does with a certain indefinable . . . Tel-ness. His myriad qualities can be broken down into the following areas:

RIBALDRY:
Tel is a red-blooded male. As much as he is civilised and restrained in the company of a refined lady like Gabby Logan, he can also engage in a bit of risqué banter when the occasion demands. Freddie Ljungberg is very much the apple of his eye:

'I do like Freddie. I like a saucy player and he is a saucy player.'

One wonders if it was Freddie who performed this act, which greatly pleased Tel:

'He's just tickled it around the corner between his legs.'

SOPHISTRY:
But Tel is nothing if not an intellectual:

'I've been asked that question for the last six months. It is not fair to expect me to make such a fast decision on something that has been put upon me like that.'

They say that it takes an intelligent individual to be able to believe two contradictory things at the same time. This would make Tel an Einsteinian genius. Don't believe us?

'It may have been going wide, but nevertheless it was a great shot on target.'

Tel is wide of the mark here, and yet strangely on target.

'They didn't change positions . . . they just moved the players around.'

Tel doesn't make statements . . . he just moves words around.

'Those are the sort of doors that get opened if you don't close them.'

Tel tends to open his trap if you don't shut it.

He can also believe the same thing twice, if you see what we mean . . .

'If history is going to repeat itself I should think we can expect the same thing again.'

If history repeats itself, we can probably expect a lot more nonsense from Tel in years to come.

'It's understandable and I understand that.'

If only we could believe you, Tel . . .

OPTIMISM / PESSIMISM:

It takes a certain kind of optimism to go into a recording studio and try to out-sing Frank Sinatra on 'I Got You Under My Skin'. So it's abundantly clear that Tel is a profoundly optimistic man.

He certainly believes he's a popular kind of guy:

'Certain people are for me, certain people are pro me.'

But on the other hand, Tel also sees the other side of the coin:

'As soon as you think you've turned the corner, you end up hitting something coming around that corner.'

SENSITIVITY:

Tel is a sensitive fellow, in touch with his own feelings, considerate of others:

'If a player has problems, he should sort them out quietly behind closed doors. If Dacourt plans to go to Italy, I'll drive him there myself.'

As touching a show of concern as you are ever likely to encounter.

And how about this for a show of solidarity after Terry Fenwick's drink-driving charge?

'The spirit he has shown has been second to none.'

But sometimes, as Tel knows, tough love is the best approach:

'If you can't stand the heat in the dressing-room, get out of the kitchen.'

FOOTBALLING NOUS:

It's the whole area of sheer honest-to-goodness football nous that is Tel's strongest suit:

'There are two ways of getting the ball. One is from your own teammates, and that's the only way.'

Tackling is for losers:

'If you can't outplay the opposition, you must outnumber them.'

Fielding 12, 13 or even 14 players can reap dividends.

'You either win or you lose. There's no in between.'

Only decades in the game can teach you things like this.

'Apart from their goals, Norway wouldn't have scored.'

Irrefutable wisdom.

'The mere fact that he's injured stops him getting injured again, if you know what I mean.'

If only every player would get injured – then there would be no injuries.

☆Barry Venison

In a nutshell: Punditry's answer to Pat Sharpe.
Gaffta Panel Verdict: Guff paled alongside garish attire.

Image-conscious sometime Sunderland and Liverpool player Barry Venison has looked to DJ Pat Sharpe throughout the past 20 years as a style template. How else to explain the evolution from ambitious blond-highlighted 1980s mullet to the equally ambitious starched short-back-and-sides of today? Never one to make an interesting comment when a boring one would do instead, Venison has nevertheless come up with a few guff gems over the years:

'The teams at the bottom of the Premiership are conceding lots of goals, and that's no coincidence.'
All pundits should pay such close attention to league statistics.

'Tempo, now there's a big word.'
What a fine vocabulary Barry has.

'The Newcastle back three, back four, back five have been at sixes and sevens.'
Barry Venison, numbers man.

'It's got nothing to do with his ability. In fact, it has got to do with his ability.'
He's nothing if not decisive.

'Henry is in what I like to call a purple patch at the moment.'
This one recalls Andy Gray's comment about 'what I like to call those "indefensible ones" – you can't defend against them'. It's the true mark of the jaded hack to pluck a stock term out of the air and claim you invented it.

'That's a 14–15 pointer there if there ever was one.'
There never was one, Barry.

'The Croatians don't play well without the ball.'
Barry spots the Croatian Achilles heel.

'Romania are more Portuguese than German.'
This is probably news to all three nationalities.

'PSV have got a lot of pace up front. They're capable of exposing themselves.'
Let's hope they leave that to the streakers, Barry.

And, of course, the all-time Venison classic:
'I always used to put my right boot on first, and then obviously my right sock.'
Obviously.

☆Ray Houghton

In a nutshell: Diminutive faux-Irish stater of the obvious.
Gaffta Panel Verdict: By dint of the breadth of his media exposure, a real contender.

Who are you, sir?
'The third smallest professional footballer in modern times. I shot to prominence in 1988 after finishing off a stylish ten-man move as Eire – though taking part in the sport for the first time – gained a surprise victory over England.'

But you're Scottish, aren't you?
'Not at all. I'm fiercely proud of my Tipperary upbringing, but in public affect a broad Scottish accent in a vain bid to deflect the spotlight.'

Of course. You're a modest fellow. We recall a quote about Fabrizio Ravanelli that shows your bashful side nicely:
'I wasn't one of his best lovers.'

So, what's your guff claim to fame then?
'Well, I'm employed by almost as many media organisations as Lawro, and my inclusion of the informative phrase "At this point in time" 39 times in a single broadcast will take some beating.'

Impressive. Let's root through the rest of your CV. We see you're noted for the clinical, acerbic eye you bring to a post-match inquest:
'This is the first goal, for me.'

You certainly came down hard on Crystal Palace a few years back:
'They've won about 20 and lost about 19, so they seem to be a bit inconsistent.'

And we can't remember anyone else who's so shrewdly cut to the heart of the Geordies' problems:
'Newcastle have struggled to score goals on their travels, especially away from home.'

As far as we recall, you had some novel ideas for getting your adopted country out of the hole Keano left them in:
'Ireland should be allowed to draft in a replacement for Keane because he must have an injury of the brain.'

Not so sure about those rumours you put round about Damien Duff though:
'He's on the lips of every team in world football.'

And you've always got a Ronglish dictionary handy, too:
'You don't want to be going out with an easy-oasy side.'

Although maybe not an English dictionary:
'See how Middlesbrough had only one up front – that was systematic of the game.'

'If he'd taken that, it could have changed the whole complexity of the match.'

Pity you've broken that abacus too:
'If there's one thing Gus Uhlenbeek's got, it's pace and determination.'

It got you through many a broadcast:
'Martin Butler's on 99 goals as well, one for the hundred.'

You might need a new watch too, come to think of it:
'Last year you could set your watch by the Liverpool back four – right-back, two centre-halves, left-back.'

You've earned quite a reputation for yourself as a radio presenter too. A man for the hard questions, we believe?
'So have you [Brian Tinnion] been involved in many games like this, where you're 4–2 down with three minutes to go and end up winning 5–4?'

That radio gig went well all round really. Suppose it helps, having such a sound grasp of business and marketing principles as well as football:
Adrian Durham: Northwich will be sharing next season with Witton Albion at the Bargain Booze Stadium.
Razor: Where do they get these names from?
Durham: I think they get a bit of money for it.
Razor: What happens when they change the sponsors, do they change the name of the stadium?
Razor sharp!

☆Ally McCoist
In a nutshell: Tiresome joker in punditry pack.
Gaffta Panel Verdict: An award might only encourage him.

Cheeky chappy Scot who has built his career as a housewives' favourite on being funnier than John Parrott, more knowledgeable than Robbie Earle and sexier than Clive Allen. Rarely funny, knowledgeable, or – one would imagine – sexy, though close admirers do describe him as the 'eighth wonder'.

The possibility of 'Coisty' making it as a serious pundit was probably over from the moment he was passed over for Andy Townsend as the driver of ITV's ill-fated *Tactics*

Truck, and certainly once he recorded a version of 'Donald, Where's Your Troosers?' that's just as depressing as you're imagining.

Instead, in lieu of having anything interesting to say about football, he plays Sid James to Robbie Earle's Joan Sims on various ITV panels.

'His best position . . . heh, heh, that'd be telling, Des, ho ho, know what I mean, Andy?'

THE McCOIST GUFFBANK:

On Jan Koller:
'Sometimes, he looks like he's towing a caravan.'

On Roy Keane and Alf-Inge Haaland:
'If he's admitted he went out to do him, he hasn't got a leg to stand on.'

Striker turned right-winger?
'When foreigners come into this country, I like to see them earning their money.'

Knowing his mind:
'Real Madrid are probably, without doubt, the best team in the world . . .'

The old chestnut:
'One thing about Germany – they'll be organised, they'll be big and they'll be strong.'

On the danger of complacency:
'Sometimes, at the back of your head, you take your foot off the gasometer.'

Celtic fans probably put it best:
'There's only one John Parrott.'

☆John Aldridge

In a nutshell: Struggling Scouser opted for adopted country to boost profile.

Gaffta Panel Verdict: Huge guff potential if given right stage.

There are cynics who say that John Aldridge only turned Irish because he had precious little chance of making the England team. Cynics of the punditry and guff game make a similar claim in terms of the Scouser's post-football career . . . he's a regular fixture on Ireland's TV3, seemingly more valued in the land of his fathers, er, grandmother, than in England.

Having packed in the manager post at Tranmere, Aldo put his best foot forward and tried to make it in the media. Sadly, Aldo's relative inarticulacy has meant that foot more often than not ended up in his own mouth – sometimes with spectaculative (as he'd say himself) effect.

But foot in mouth hasn't been Aldo's only problem. His relative lack of headway has largely been as a result of his attempt to gain a foothold in the most competitive department of the punditry game – that of the ex-Liverpool player brigade.

How Aldo must curse the likes of Lawro and Beglin – two former Reds who've beaten him to the punch by virtue of having their on-pitch careers prematurely ended through injury. Foolishly, Aldridge allowed his football career to run into his late 30s, a time when he should have been working on his media persona.

Aldridge has been unable to make up lost ground. At every turn, he is thwarted by former Liverpool FC players. Lawro fills every available gap at the Beeb. Beglin has more than a foothold on ITV and the main Irish national broadcaster RTE. Spackman, Houghton, Neal, Walsh, McMahon and Whelan tussle with him for airtime in Sky's reserves (watching pointless Carling Cup matches on a Tuesday or Wednesday night).

The Scouser's one regular gig is on the aforementioned TV3. Aldridge is essentially still on Sky's books, but he has been loaned out to the Irish outfit to gain experience. Sky are clearly hoping to unearth the new John Parrot. But it's a chance to impress that Aldo has failed to grasp – and he now seems to have little chance of ever ousting the morose Stapo from Sky's coverage of Ireland matches.

Inarticulacy and tough competition are major problems for John, but as it happens, they are not the critical factor – after all Paul Walsh gets regular TV work. No, John's biggest problem is of a different order and somewhat more difficult to rectify. Having built his football career on his striking physical resemblance to Ian Rush, Aldo's media career has ironically been stultified because he is also imbued – nay, afflicted – with the great Welshman's televisual persona.

THE ALDO GUFFBANK:
'Last week's match was a real game of cat and dog.'

'There's only one team in Europe you can leave Manchester United for – and that's Real Madrid or Barcelona.'

'In years gone by, Arsenal have kicked themselves in the foot many times.'

'It won't be the first substitution he'll make tonight.'

'Maybe with 25 minutes left, they'll introduce [*sic*] Fowler.'

☆Alan Hansen
In a nutshell: Lounging atop the punditry tree like the cat that got the cream.
Gaffta Panel Verdict: Just going through the motions.

(a) Absolutely magnificent. Pace. Power. Control. Possession. Movement. It had everything.

(b) Absolutely diabolical. Nobody picking up. Nobody pushing out. Nobody passing the ball. Shocking.

Look, Hansen's not putting much effort in so why should we? He can be summed up thus.

1. Play a bit
2. Dress only in black
3. Somehow cultivate reputation as thinking man's pundit
4. Secure job for life on Beeb
5. Take foot entirely off pedal
6. Dress how you like
7. Choose (a) or (b) above
8. Repeat to fade

THE HANSEN GUFFBANK:

'The proof of the pudding – is in the second-half performance.'

'You wouldn't be surprised if England went on and won 9–0.'
Actually, we'd have been very surprised, since the score was 2–2 at the time.

On a Coventry–Spurs cup draw:
'Potential potato skin there.'

Expert opinion:
'What you don't want to do against United is go behind.'

WINNER

☆ Mark Lawrenson

In a nutshell: Versatile, pun-obsessed dandy bounced back well from 'tache loss.

Gaffta Panel Verdict: Has stepped up a gear since Ron departed.

Lawro is the chameleon of the guff game. A curiously dapper centre-half by trade, he still managed to turn out in just about every other position on the pitch for Liverpool and Ireland. Likewise, he now plies his eloquent brand of punditry with at least 400 different media organisations, saving his big performances for Ray Stubbs' couch and then sleepwalking through a host of outings for Irish radio, press and telly.

Unfortunately for his myriad employers, this 'game as a pebble' try-anything-once attitude has translated to Lawro frequently trying out words and phrases with which he has only made the vaguest acquaintance.

Thus Gary Neville becomes . . .
'. . . palpable for the second goal'

Burnley getting beat will . . .
'. . . stick in their claw'

Fabien Barthez tends to . . .
'. . . fall between two schools'

Manchester United, in general, seem to have a . . .
'. . . dirge of central defenders'

resulting, inevitably, in them . . .
'. . . decapitating against Stuttgart'.

To be fair to Lawro, however, at least he's not one of those pundits who shouts the odds without ever having had a go at the management lark himself. An eventful spell in charge at Oxford United left him with only one real regret:

'Not pushing Robert Maxwell off his boat.'

However, his dealings with Big Bob rather put him off being a gaffer, and apart from a brief spell vainly attempting to persuade Kevin Keegan's Newcastle to consider defending, he threw his hat – velvet trilby, one imagines – into the punditry ring.

Listening to Lawro, perhaps it's just as well he chose the gantry over the dugout.

That Newcastle gig was always a non-starter:

'It's sometimes easier to defend a one-goal lead than a two-goal lead.'

It's doubtful if he could really bring out the best in a side:

'Ireland will always give 99 per cent – everything they've got.'

He's always had trouble with formations:

'It looks like they'll be playing 4–4–1–2.'

Of course, although it might say 'pundit' on his passport, Lawro is really a burgeoning comedian, simply using his ample BBC airtime to hone his act before hawking it around Merseyside's working men's clubs.

Ray Stubbs and Barry Davies, in particular, are willing foils.

Stubbsy: What's been missing from Liverpool's play during this run of 1 point from 15?
Lawro: Wins.

Davies: I think you'll recall he [Canizares] missed the World Cup through dropping a bottle of aftershave on his foot.
Lawro: He also missed out on a move to Cologne.

Stubbsy: I believe Gérard Houllier misses today's game with vomiting and diarrhoea.
Lawro: He's not got gastroenteritis. He's just got a bad side.

Indeed, much of Stubbsy and Lawro's analysis seems to be little more than a pun-off:
Stubbs: Will Greece lightning strike twice in the final?
Lawro: Not unless the referee is going to be a Homer.

And as if a promising stand-up career wasn't enough, Lawro also seems keen to capitalise on Big Ron's gantry exile to grab a slice of football's prestigious Dialect Development action. With Ronglish in cold storage, Lawro has been working overtime on the building blocks of Lawrgo – a primitive enough means of communication almost entirely based on rhyming slang.

And so a wild shot blazed high over the bar becomes . . .
'. . . pound of bacon, lean back . . .'

a tired old veteran goes down late in the game with . . .
'. . . a bit of rising damp . . .'

and a keeper's dodgy handling gives rise to the less-than-liturgically accurate . . .
'. . . pat-a-cake, pat-a-cake *butcher's* man.'

Even more sneakily, Lawro has begun to claim more and more Ronglish staples as his own.

All of a sudden, anyone not giving it the full 99 per cent has become . . .
'. . . a little bit easy-oasy . . .'

any manner of mild inconvenience now is . . .
'. . . a big ask . . .'

all unconvincing goalkeepers have developed . . .
'. . . a chocolate wrist . . .'

185

and, worst of all, Ron's intimate knowledge of alternative geology is invoked every time a team goes on a bad run . . .
'Bolton have halted their slide down the glass mountain.'

Whatever the old chancer's faults, however, we probably should just be glad to have Lawro still performing at his nonsensical peak. A couple of years ago, a shudder rippled through the guff world when a wager gone wrong saw Lawro shorn of his trademark moustache. Emerging from the gruelling 12-hour operation a slightly less dandy individual, many worried that, like Samson, Lawro had been stripped of his guff powers.

We need not have concerned ourselves. If anything, he's going from strength to strength.
'Kilbane's like a one-eyed cat in a fish shop – he doesn't know what to do or where to go.'

'The qualification was the big thing – they've doubled that!'

'They're in pole position, i.e. third position, for the Champions League.'

'These managers all know their onions and cut their cloth accordingly.'

'Liverpool have finished fourth, third and second, so if they finish fifth it'll be an average season for them.'

'If Mick gets an offer from a Premiership team, I've said it tomorrow in the newspaper, he'll go.'

'He [Veron] can sometimes be the icing on the cake, but other times he's the . . . umm . . . piece underneath that nobody sees.'

'Classic own goal from Michael Jackson. Bet he didn't do that in rehearsal. Tell you what, if you were his manager, you'd tell him to beat it. Wasn't a thriller.'

'It's like the Sea of Galilee – the two defenders just parted.'

'It was a foul but it didn't need to constitute five rollovers, did it? Thought it was a lottery draw for a minute.'

THE CARRY-ON COMMENTATING AWARD

10 'PSV have got a lot of pace up front. They're capable of exposing themselves.'
Barry Venison

9. 'He was under a lot of pressure because we were going to give him one if he didn't come up to scratch.'
Lawro on Dion Dublin

8. 'He's gone too erect, no shape there, and there she goes.'
Noel King on some scrappy midfield action.

7. 'Pahars is imminent. He's stripped off and ready to come.'
Clive Tyldesley

6. 'The Europeans just have to feel you and they will go down.'
Dennis Irwin

5. 'Plenty to get your mouth round on the Burnley bench: Michopoulos . . . Papadopoulos . . . Little . . . Cox.'
Peter Morris on BBC Berks

4. 'Ronaldo throws the leg over four or five times but he doesn't produce anything.'
Ronnie Whelan

3. 'Danny Murphy's been scoring with benders all season.'
Bryan Robson

2. 'For such a small man Maradona gets great elevation on his balls.'
David Pleat

1. 'McCarthy gave Ian Harte a special cuddle after he pulled him off.'
Barry Davies

THE RADIO GA-GA AWARD

'Did you see me on the radio?' Irish jockey Tony Dobbin once wondered, after a handsome win at Cheltenham. And there, as they say, is the rub. Flawed appliance that the wireless surely is, we didn't. Worse still, we could hear him perfectly.

They say a picture paints a thousand words. And while there are many that wish the likes of Motty would take greater heed of the maxim, it stands to reason that your average radio commentator or pundit must be called upon to produce added verbiage by the ton in lieu of pictorial evidence. Little wonder, then, that the radio was once the spiritual home of guff.

It certainly produced the landmark sporting gaffe of our time. The England v. West Indies Test series of 1976 provided the backdrop. Brian Johnston was at the mic and Peter Willey and Michael Holding were poised at the crease. The likes of David Baddiel will die trying before they could write what followed:

'The bowler's Holding, the batsman's Willey.'

While living up to those standards represents – as they'd say themselves – a big ask, the football commentators have not been slow to step up to the plate. You've got cranky Alan Green, excitable Jonathan Pearce, sensible Mick Ingham and lyrical Stuart Hall and his jockstraps full of dynamite. And then there's a little-known Mancunian nonsense factory that blows everyone away. Just wait and see.

In *Fever Pitch*, Nick Hornby described listening to football on the radio thus:

'Football reduced to its lowest common denominator. Shorn of the game's aesthetic pleasures, or the comfort of the crowd that feels the same way as you, or the sense of security that you get when you see that your defenders and your goalkeeper are more or less where they should be, all that is left is naked fear.'

He was nearly right. Fear and guff.

THE ALSO-RANS

☆Stuart Hall
In a nutshell: The only known guffster to painstakingly script his output.
Gaffta Panel Verdict: Was almost disqualified entirely for trying too hard.

'Brian Deane has dynamite in his jockstrap!'

'Dunne's anaconda thighs were no match for Wright-Phillips' sinewy limbs.'

'What will you do when you leave football, Jack – will you stay in football?'

☆ Jimmy Armfield

In a nutshell: Veteran guff merchant. Will do a job for you.
Gaffta Panel Verdict: Howard Wilkinson didn't know who he was. Sadly, nor do the youth of today.

'He's only a foot away from the linesman – or should I say a metre, in modern parlance.'
No, Jimmy, you shouldn't.

'With eight minutes left, the game could be won in the next five or ten minutes.'

'I'd like to have seen Tony Morley left on as a down-and-out winger.'

'I think that their young legs would have found younger hearts inside them.'

☆ Alan Brazil

In a nutshell: Ex-Man U frontman turned TalkSport host.
Gaffta Panel Verdict: Unfortunately, Al has to share guff limelight with sidekick Mike Parry.

'No European nation has won back-to-back European Championships.'

'Our talking point this morning is George Best, his liver transplant and the booze culture in football. Don't forget, the best caller wins a crate of John Smith's.'

And unforgettably . . .
Al: I was sad to hear yesterday about the death of Inspector Morse, TV's John Shaw.
Mike Parry: John Thaw, Alan.
Al: Do you know, I've been doing that all morning. John, if you're listening, sorry, mate.

☆Stan Collymore

In a nutshell: Contrary frontman who lifted depression with a stint on the Beeb.

Gaffta Panel Verdict: Fledgling guff career 'dogged' by controversy.

'The panic bells are ringing at Boro at the moment.'

'He sticks his backside into the defender, makes sure he can move him, makes sure he's pliable.'

'From where I'm from, that was offside.'

☆Bryon Butler

In a nutshell: Sadly deceased king of the match report.

Gaffta Panel Verdict: Won't indict him when he's not around to defend himself.

'Fifty thousand here tonight, but it sounds like fifty-two thousand.'

'That now means that from the British point of view, Anderlecht lead 3–2.'

'Butcher goes forward as Ipswich throw their last trump card into the fire.'

☆Peter Jones

In a nutshell: Another of the Beeb's voices of record.

Gaffta Panel Verdict: Even the most distinguished have their moments.

'They're floating up on a sea of euphoria, and hoping to drag themselves clear of the quicksand at the bottom.'

'Sporting Lisbon in their green and white hoops, looking like a team of zebras.'

'Arsenal now have plenty of time to dictate the last few seconds.'

'Ian Rush is deadly ten times out of ten, but that wasn't one of them.'

☆Ron Jones
In a nutshell: Another BBC legend recently on loan to Irish station Today FM.
Gaffta Panel Verdict: Sharp as a flash.

'And Rush, quick as a needle.'

'Now Zola tries to inject some speed.'

'You felt this was the sort of game that needed a goal to break the deadlock.'

THE NOMINEES

☆Jonathan Pearce
In a nutshell: Frustrated stand-up does robot and football voicing.
Gaffta Panel Verdict: It's not guff when it's deliberate.

Perhaps the loudest, most excitable commentator currently operating in English football.

For every time we've had a chuckle at a South American mic-man who's roared 'Goaaaalllllll' for five minutes after Carlos Kickaball manages to notch, you suspect that Buenos Aires's answer to Helen Chamberlain is splitting her sides over old Channel Five footage of Pearce beside himself after a near-miss during a classic Zenith Data Systems cup tie.

Still, admirable as his excitement might be, one has to remain slightly suspicious of someone whose excited frenzy when commentating on Steel Avenger v. Wheely Big Cheese for *Robot Wars* is indistinguishable from that which he would whip up for England v. Germany in the World Cup final. Could Jonathan – whisper it – be faking it?

By the way, while we're on the subject, *Robot Wars* (for the uninitiated, a BBC show on which lumps of misshapen metal are repeatedly driven into one another by nerdy youths with remote controls until one or both 'robots' ceases to function) at least nails the lie that it's only unfortunate football commentators who are subjected to the unceasing wrath of know-it-all Joe Public.

For while browsing the Information Superhighway for details of Pearce's side-earner, we found stinging criticism of his *Robot Wars* commentary style. Apparently, Pearcey 'doesn't know the difference between hydraulics and pneumatics'. Much like Ally McCoist and the offside law, he cares little for the complex rules governing techno-jousts; he can't spot whether a robot is jammed or is simply 'grounded on its armour'. Most shamefully, he is 'perpetually sure that a flywheel weapon has broken just because it stops when it's hit something'. And to think Jonathan thought he got a hard time from Tottenham fans. Anyhow, whether Jonathan is faking it or not, he's certainly not afraid to give himself up to the moment. A rudimentary enough Paul Merson free-kick during a run-of-the-mill European tie at Highbury produced this famous Pearce outburst:

'Merson bends the ball round the WAAAALLLL! OOOOOHHHHH, HOCUS-POCUS! Magic-man Merson: hubble bubble . . . loads of trouble: Standard Liege.'

And his reaction to England's shootout victory over Spain in Euro 1996 was no bedfellow of restraint, dignity or decorum:

'Salvador Dali, Pablo Picasso, José Carreras, El Cordobes, Don Quixote. Your boys are out and England are through! And you can stick it up your Julio Iglesi-arse.'

Of course, Pearce is very much the Nicky Barmby of the gantry – so far, he has hawked his talents to the Beeb, Sky, Capital Gold and Five. And just as Barmby always seems to fill his pockets, however miserable the gig, Pearce is not afraid to tip the cap to his paymasters:

'It's tight and tense – almost as tight and tense as Channel 5's film _Get Carter_, which follows this match.'

Of course, Pearce's most famous piece of commentary/advertising left rather a bitter taste:

'Welcome to Bologna on Capital Gold for England v. San Marino with Tennent's Pilsner, brewed with Czechoslovakian yeast for that extra Pilsner taste, and England are one down.'

Generously, though, Pearce doesn't charge an extra penny for lacing his commentaries with highbrow flights of fancy inspired by his keen interest in all forms of art and culture.

Reminiscing about dodgy '60s sci-fi is a particularly relaxing way of whiling away an Upton Park bore draw:

'West Ham's light blue and claret away kit was a classic . . . I remember having a team of Subbuteo players in those colours. I bet half of our listeners don't even know what Subbuteo is. Well, if you were a boy growing up in the late 1960s, that was all there was to keep you going, that and _Barbarella_, with Jane Fonda . . . er . . . and here, with a Barbarella-style haircut, comes Ray Parlour now.'

And where would Jonathan be without Yogi?

'And it's 2–0 to the USA. Is that a mistake? Is it a boo-boo? No, because the USA are smarter than the average bear at this World Cup!'

He was a firm believer that the boy Astaire was lightning over the first five yards:

'Van Nistelrooy! Oh, what a goal! He jinked, he wriggled, he danced . . . faster than Fred Astaire at his best!'

And he may even have read the odd book or two:

'And Wright twisted and turned, twisted and turned . . . there were more twists than an Agatha Christie novel and more turns than Hampton Court bleeding maze.'

Don't be fooled for a second by that nice-guy image, however. Pearce can kill a man with his bare mic. Many's the hapless Geordie defender who has had his reputation mortally wounded:

'I wouldn't trust Newcastle's back five to protect my garden gnomes from squirrels.'

Nor do misfiring strikers escape unscathed:

'The Arsenal strikers are scrabbling around the box like children round a Christmas tree. But the presents weren't there and Santa hadn't come.'

And he produced this particularly fine moment during a UEFA cup tie in Norway:

'So, in this land of trolls, Dennis Wise will take the corner for Chelsea.'

Even the Pearce gaffes have a certain lyrical quality:

'When you're down, you Palace fans, the fickle finger of fate rarely smiles on you.'

Well maybe not all of them:

'All of Liverpool's away wins against Tottenham in the Premier League this year have been at White Hart Lane.'

'Vialli's absolutely certain that he knows one way or the other whether he'll score or not.'

'And Chapman is charging around like a dinosaur. I wonder what Frank McClintock thinks – he's our one for the history.'

Sadly, Pearce broke his leg as a teenage trialist with Bristol City and never recovered sufficiently to make a professional career in the game. If it's any consolation to him, he should know that whatever he might have achieved in the game, it could scarcely have matched the simple magnificence of his greatest commentating feat.

It was another Arsenal Cup-Winner's Cup tie on Capital Gold. Paul Merson was on the ball again. This time, Sampdoria defender Riccardo Ferri unceremoniously brought him down. Pearce had his cue . . . his stage . . . his finest hour . . .

'It was Ferri across the Merson.'
Stand and applaud.

☆Alan Green

In a nutshell: Irritable Irish Five Live mainstay.
Gaffta Panel Verdict: Would only upset people at awards bash.

Greenie is one of BBC Five Live's top football commentator big guns. Born in Belfast, Green has become a kind of commentating equivalent of Terry Wogan. He generally gets the gig when England are in action, and while the accent may have the Irish lilt, the boxers are certainly of the order of the cross of St George. It's like listening to Terry at the Eurovision.

According to the BBC website profile, Greenie is an avid football fan, seeing more than 100 matches a season. Perhaps this is because he is paid to do so? Anyway, Green is something of a trailblazer in commentary terms – having developed a reputation for calling a spade a spade and a poor match awful. Of course, it's easier to do this when working for a public service broadcaster! Sadly, however, Green's 'honest and uncompromising assessment of the game' has become something of a bore over time. He needs a new gimmick.

For those who are interested in this type of thing, according to the BBC site, Green is married with two children and lives in Cheshire.

THE GREEN GUFFBANK:

'It was the game that put the Everton ship back on the road.'

'This will be their 19th consecutive game without a win unless they can get an equaliser.'

'John Moncur has been much more effective since he came on.'

'Xavier, who looks just like Zeus, not that I have any idea what Zeus looks like.'

'You don't score 64 goals in 86 games without being able to score goals.'

'Tugay is writhing around all over the place as if he were dead.'

'They care about their club, and that's why they always have something good to say, even when it is negative.'

'Ziege hits it high for Heskey who isn't playing.'

'His official height is 5 ft 5 in. and he doesn't look much taller than that.'

And the bloodthirsty:
'John Arne Riise was deservedly blown up for that foul.'

☆ Mike Ingham

In a nutshell: Takes turns at the mic with Green. Usually too smooth for guff.

Gaffta Panel Verdict: Greek Euro win a career highlight.

Ingham is Five Live's thinking man's commentator – exuding a manner of calm, collected consideration. Generally paired in big games with Alan Green – he provides dignified balance to the excitable, opinionated Irishman. The pairing tends to work well, with Ingham clearly positioned by Auntie with mic primed to thump the histrionics out of the little round Irishman, should he become too animated.

Ingham is what the Beeb is all about – as a broadcaster he's the acceptable voice of that green and pleasant land, the quintessential English gent, the kind of stock that built an empire. Sadly, because he's actually a very good commentator, guff and nonsense can be hard to come by – consequently, he doesn't compare favourably against other gantry guff giants.

THE INGHAM GUFFBANK:

'. . . evoking memories, particularly of days gone by.'

'Martin O'Neill, standing, hands on hips, stroking his chin.'

'Neil Sullivan has stopped absolutely everything they have thrown at him . . . Wimbledon 1, Manchester United 1.'

'Tottenham are trying tonight to become the first London team to win this cup. The last team to do so was the 1973 Spurs team.'

And as Zagorakis lifted the Euro 2004 trophy for Greece, Mike rather lost the run of himself:

'There'll be no more grey days. It's Grecian 2004!!!'

☆Conor McNamara

In a nutshell: Recent BBC Irish signing.

Gaffta Panel Verdict: Staking his guff claim at a tender age. Set to be a major contender for future awards.

> 'This was like the Steven Spielberg movie, *Catch Me If You Can*. It was about two mice who fell into a bowl of cream, one kept going and thrashing around until the cream turned to butter and the harder surface enabled him to clamber out. Mind you, Sam Allardyce will wonder about the defending for the equaliser. Three blind mice more like.'

He might not yet be one of the main players in the guff game, but mark our words, Conor Mac is one for the future. Still a largely unremarkable presence at BBC Five Live, where he cuts his teeth on the fixtures that Green, Ingham and co. don't fancy, Premiership match reports like the above occasionally showcase clear designs on Stuart Hall's throne.

And Conor has form. The first one of their number to make the break into respectable employment, he is an honours graduate of the nonsense finishing school that is Irish TV station TV3. Perhaps the highlight of his schooling was an infamous attempt to explain away a substantial period of added time during a Champions League clash between Liverpool and Boavista:

> 'The trainers weren't on the pitch at all . . . but, of course, the referee does have to take into account the minute's silence.'

The only surprise was the ref failed to add anything for the time wasted during the players' warm-up, not to mention 20 minutes or so to compensate for his pre-game bath.

Conor is the son of legendary Irish radio DJ Micky Mac and has inherited all of his oul' fella's chirpiness – or capacity to irritate:

'What United have unleashed at Old Trafford tonight they hope will take them all the way to the . . . land of the trophy.'

Of course he still has a bit of learning to do. The complexities of a two-legged European tie sometimes confuse Conor:

'The longer the score stays at 0–0 the better for Barcelona. Remember, if they can score next week, it will be an away goal.'

Fair enough, but wouldn't Barca be even better off if they actually scored a goal at home, too? Sure enough, the Catalans would eventually regret their reticence – rather taking a blunt instrument to the task of getting that away goal:

'Barcelona are desperately looking for a hole with which to pierce the Liverpool rearguard.'

To his credit, Conor was as surprised as anyone when an inexperienced referee failed to consult his amended Manchester United rulebook:

'That foul by Silvestre was deemed to be illegal.'

And sometimes, he hit the nail plum square on the head:

'Liverpool playing with a bit of a swagger now, emphasised by that flick by Heskey which went out of play.'

One of his final acts at TV3 was this landmark slice of oxymoronical guff:

'They say football is unscripted drama and this match certainly hasn't followed the script tonight.'

As profound as it is nonsensical? We doubt it. Keep an eye on this fella.

☆Tony Cascarino

In a nutshell: Mystery he made it as a player. Bigger mystery he's making it on the radio.

Gaffta Panel Verdict: TalkSport slot a guff goldmine, but perhaps it's as good as it gets for Tone.

To be honest, Tony Cascarino has made it through on potential alone. We've heard enough from him to believe he can cut it amongst the guff big boys, but it will take stronger constitutions than ours to endure his drive-time show on TalkSport in order to compile the evidence.

Anyhow, in fairness to the big fella, he should be an inspiration to us all. In his career as a professional footballer and now a professional pundit, he's shown us what we can achieve despite our limitations. In the past, Big Cas has illustrated that you don't have to be good with your feet to be a player. Now he's showing us that you don't have to be good with your mouth to work on the radio. He's also shown that you don't really have to be Irish to play for Ireland!

With two giant clubs for feet, and another for a head, Cascarino made the most of his height and bulk to become one of the most immobile target men in the game. Seldom in the goals with any great regularity, Big Cas managed to play for great clubs like Villa, Chelsea, Celtic and Marseille. He also managed to go to two World Cups with his adopted country. His career is one of football's great mysteries.

And now his career in the media appears to be progressing in similar vein. Cascarino is something of a journo/pundit – with a regular opinion piece in *The Times* as well as an anchor role on TalkSport. All this despite a general inability to express himself! Impressive.

So how has he done it? The answer lies in his rather excellent autobiography: *Full Time: The Secret Life of Tony Cascarino*. First, it's well written. Second, it's a brutally honest depiction of a rather limited footballer and an imperfect man. Ah, say you, the man has talent with the written word – no wonder *The Times* came calling. But you'd be wrong – although the story was his, the words were not. They were put in his mouth by top sports journalist Paul Kimmage – the book's ghostwriter.

Never mind, said *The Times*, the book went down so well they gave its subject a contract. (Interestingly, the ghostwriter is also an employee of the same paper.) TalkSport did likewise – looking for an opinionated co-host for its formulaic ding-dong opinion-gainsaying shows.

The newspaper contract is the least strange of Cas's two jobs – after all, you can employ someone to put Cas's thoughts on paper in a tidy fashion. But the same can't be said for the radio slot, where Cas gives hope to all those with marbles in their mouths who dream of employment in broadcasting!

Cas is an up-and-comer in the guff game. His career is only in its infancy. But with a three-hour slot daily on the airwaves, his potential for future Gaffta nominations is as big as his size fourteens!

THE BIG CAS GUFFBANK:

'Many tournament hosts have done well in the past. The obvious example is Denmark in 1992 – who were more or less at home.'
Tony brings Swedish sovereignty into question.

'Roy Keane didn't go through the book with a fine toothbrush.'

'I expect Chelsea to make a world-record signing in the near distant future.'

'That guy Van Nistelrooy, he's a great number 9.'
Cas, just as a TV camera focused on the back of United's great number 10.

'When I first arrived at Marseille, Bernard Tapie [then the club's owner] said to me: "I don't like Lee Chapman. I didn't like Mark Hateley. I like players like Chris Waddle." I thought, oh shit, what am I doing here?'

'Paul Elliott arrived in our dressing-room wearing an immaculate leather trenchcoat. Hoddle raced to the "cover" of a bin in the corner and started shooting him with imaginary bullets – "Pshhhh, Pshhhh" – like a five year old with a cowboy pistol set. What Paul didn't realise was that Glenn was trying to be funny, and when Glenn tried to be funny it was time to pass around the laughing gas – he was probably the unfunniest man I have ever known.'

WINNER

☆ Tom Tyrrell

In a nutshell: The voice of Manchester United.
Gaffta Panel Verdict: A one-man guff industry. Magnificent.

Those of you unfamiliar with north-west local radio, or Irish station Today FM, may be blissfully unaware of the one-man nonsense production facility that is Tom Tyrrell.

So perhaps a random selection of choice cuts from the Tyrrell CV might give you some idea what kind of character we're dealing with here.

- Tom has spent some time as the stadium announcer at Old Trafford.
- He is the author of *The Illustrated History of Manchester United*.
- Finding his writing style particularly suitable to the

more visual tome, Tom also tackled the bits between the pictures in *The Illustrated Cantona*.

- He also gave David Meek a hand with *Manchester United in Europe*: *The Complete Journey, 1956–2001*.
- And finally, he is the author – and possibly a leading evangelist of – *Manchester United: The Religion*.

Yes, you've got the picture. Red Tom is radio's answer to Clive Tyldesley. When he's not tucked up in his Keano duvet or swapping his spare Giggsy stickers to fill his United Panini album, Tom is usually commentating on his heroes for one broadcaster or another. If United are away, he might venture as far as Bolton or maybe even Elland Road. Occasionally, he'll glumly go through the motions covering Man City or Blackburn. He has never been spotted south of Birmingham.

Like Clive, Tom makes little effort to hide his allegiance. In his mind, he has awarded Ruud van Nistelrooy more penalties than even Mike Riley. In charging to the rescue of Gary Neville or Wes Brown, he has screamed for offside more often than Tony Adams and Steve Bould combined. And only Ron and Clive have excused more scything Paul Scholes tackles as 'slightly mistimed'.

Such is Tom's obsession with all things United that even when success on the pitch temporarily deserts his faves, Tom will find a way to revel in the small victories:

'Against Arsenal, West Brom had a corner after ten seconds, but there's ten seconds gone now and they still haven't had a corner, so United can say they've had a better start than Arsenal.'

His obsession with the men of Trafford aside, however, none of Tom's excitable Premiership commentaries are complete without the following ten staples.

1. BLOODLUST

Tom is an old-school gent. Normally paired with similarly long-toothed pundits like David Fairclough or Mick Martin, the afternoon is usually spent moaning about how football has become 'non-contact' and surmising that some of the foreigners on view 'still don't like it up 'em'.

It always cheers Tom a little when a midfield assassin leaves the foot in:

'It wasn't a terrible foul, but it was quite exciting the way he came in and took his man.'

Even better if one of his heroes is the aggressor:

'Tremendous bad challenge by Sheringham.'

In fact, the worse the tackle the better in Tom's eyes:

'To bring down one man is good, but three, that must be a record.'

It would be thoroughly unfair, however, to suggest that Tom doesn't know the difference between right and wrong:

'The crazy thing about throwing things is that you could hit your own players. Though you shouldn't really throw things at all.'

2. ATTENTION TO DETAIL

There is no sharper eye in football than Tom's. Or no greater thirst for the kind of detail that might not necessarily be of profound importance to the listener:

'This pitch looks beautiful – mower marks, about ten yards wide, all the way up the pitch . . . well, maybe not ten yards, maybe about eight yards.'

'There's a free kick now in the box, just in that little space between the eighteen-yard line and the six-yard line, that little incomplete rectangle. I don't know what you'd call that geometrically, that three-sided rectangle.'

3. SUSPICION OF FOREIGNERS

Tom recognises no political border bar the one surrounding the Republic of Mancunia. They're all the same, these fellows:

'Great challenge by Lauren, excellent tackle by the Frenchman.'

'And speaking of Dutch total football, here's Wiltord.'

'And Pires goes through the middle, slips it into the net and it's 5–0. Actually, it was Vieira.'

4. GANTRY CRITIQUES

Every Tyrrell broadcast features a comprehensive review of the commentary position:

'I was a bit worried about the view from here because of our distance from the pitch, but it's a brilliant view. BRILLIANT! David [Fairclough] nods.'

'There's actually a hotel under here . . . you can actually stay in the private boxes . . . there are private boxes that convert to bedrooms – though not during the game of course!'

And fantastically:

'We are about as far away from the penalty box as the penalty box is from us.'

5. SCIENTIFIC APPROACH

Long before ProZone or Opta or any of these new-fangled football statistic services, Tom was providing his own precise analysis of every aspect of play:

'Mart Poom, who we have been saying is such a competent keeper, was at least 60 per cent at fault for the Liverpool goal.'

Nor were the hours spent copying his physics homework entirely wasted:

'The ball stuck to his foot like a magnet attracting a piece of steel, or metal rather.'

'Either there's a magnet behind the goal with the polarity to draw the ball away from it, or they haven't got their shooting boots on.'

Funnily enough, the humble science of basic mathematics remains an elusive skill:

'They'll close the gap on Arsenal to two points. Who knows what the gap might have been if they hadn't had that hiccup before Christmas and lost to Blackburn and Middlesbrough.'

6. DESCRIPTIVE POWERS

'Most of the play is in the middle of the pitch, like a giant Easter egg.'

As opposed to being in one team's half, like a giant Christmas cake.

'Peter Beardsley used to slide in and hit the ball with the hip – or leg that he wasn't standing on – if you get my description.'

We don't.

7. METAPHORS

In truth, Tom doesn't really do metaphors. But he tries his best:

'Owen runs like a rabbit chasing after . . . what do rabbits run after? They run after nothing . . . well, running after other rabbits.'

'Not sure what Hoddle is doing there – sticking his backside out and waving his arms about. Just like Christmas time when Dad's had too much sherry.'

'He can't turn three times, like Dick Whittington might have done . . .'

8. INFORMATION CONTENT

Tom will not help you glean what's happening in the football match at which he's supposedly present. In fact, it might not be entirely unfair to suggest that he's not actually very good at commentating:

'It's gotten so exciting I've forgotten the score. I had to look at my notes to get it right. It's 1–1!'

You can't expect Tom to count as well. What are co-commentators for, anyway?

'Great ball. Gooalll. No. Yes. Goalkick.'
Offside, Tom.

'Goallllll. No. Yes. He's given it. Has he?'
No, Tom.

9. COMMAND OF LANGUAGE

Eloquence, verbosity, lucidity. No, not Tom:
'Everybody's swinging at it. It's like those little men on twirly things you have in the pub.'

'That would have been a tremendous non-goal situation had it beaten Hoult, but the flag was up.'

'Van Nistelrooy has become a scoring phenomena.'

10. SHEER NONSENSE

There is magic amongst the madness:
'There's an old saying in football that he who scores next when it's 3–1 can influence the outcome of the game.'

'Everyone's looking to the right now. Don't know why. It's like when you stand on the street and look up at a chimney and everyone looks with you for no reason.'

'Ferdinand, with a big, long left knee, cuts that out.'

'Newcastle are finally going to end their London bogey. They haven't won there since . . . a long time ago. That would be a ghost . . . no, an albatross off their necks.'

'Kanu, who almost created the first goal minutes before it was scored.'

SERVICES TO GUFF AWARD: DAVID COLEMAN

At any decent awards ceremony, there's always a near-hysterical recipient blubbering about the one person who made everything possible. And so, as we struggle to open the Services to Guff Award envelope, please feel free to imagine a glamorous – if highly strung – honey shedding the saltiest of tears. For there is one man without whom this entire festival of nonsense could not have happened. Truly, the founding father of the sporting gaffe is none other than . . . Mr David Coleman. What about a big hand for the great man?

Coleman is, of course, the legendary BBC commentator for whom the term 'Colemanballs' was coined. Not to put too fine a point on it, David rather frequently made what could only be described as a 'balls' of his commentary. Happily, this fine sobriquet has endured to this day, now surviving as a catch-all term for all manner of commentator mishap.

Sadly, the master himself is now semi-retired, and rarely adds to his groundbreaking collection of gaffes. However, from his '60s stint as *Grandstand*'s first host, right through the *Match of the Day* years and on to *Question of Sport* (when it was watchable), Coleman's back catalogue acts as something of a template for every slow-witted mic-man that followed in his footsteps. So much so that every time you hear a new gaffe, the chances are that David made it first.

COLEMAN'S GUFF HISTORY ROADMAP:
(Note: In reproducing this invaluable historical document, we must occasionally veer momentarily from football and into Coleman's first love, the altogether different world of Track and Field.)

First recorded 'Ooh, Matron' moment. Since patented:
'There goes Juantorena down the back straight, opening his legs and showing his class.'

First commentator to acknowledge the insidious threat posed to international athletics by sexual tampering:
'And the line-up for the final of the women's 400 metres hurdles includes three Russians, two East Germans, a Pole, a Swede and a Frenchman.'

First commentator to turn back time:
'And here's Moses Kiptanui – the 19-year-old Kenyan, who turned 20 a few weeks ago.'

And first to confound physics:
'He is accelerating all the time. That last lap was run in 64 seconds and the one before in 62.'

First great sporting technique innovator since Fosbury:
'It's a great advantage to be able to hurdle with both legs.'

First commentator to spoil things for the Likely Lads:
'Don't tell those coming in now the result of that fantastic match. Now, let's have another look at Italy's winning goal.'

First with a guff genre later perfected by Motty:
'And for those of you who are watching who haven't got television sets, live commentary is on Radio 2.'

First commentator to become truly comfortable with the obvious:

'On this 102nd Cup final today, there are just two teams left.'

Mr Coleman is in no need of a dictionary:

'The pace of the match is really accelerating, by which I mean it is getting faster all the time.'

THE REST OF THE COLEMAN GUFFBANK:

'The Republic of China: back in the Olympic Games for the first time.'

'That's the fastest time ever run, but it's not as fast as the world record.'

'There's going to be a real ding-dong when the bell goes.'

'Forest have now lost six matches without winning.'

'Both of the Villa scorers were born in Liverpool. As was the Villa manager, who was born in Birkenhead.'

'The ball has broken 50–50 for Keegan.'

'Billy Hughes is like electricity – very sharp.'

'Hunter – his left foot qualifies him for the magic circle.'

'She's not Ben Johnson – but then who is?'

THE YANKS' AWARD

What is with the Americans and football? For FIFA, they are a problematic nation. For a start, to them it's called 'sawker', and involves lots of 'vertical aerial challenges', 'infield attritionals' and 'PK denials'. Second, the American populace can be divided into four categories:

- those who have no interest in football (most Americans)
- those who think it's a game for women and/or children only (most of the rest)
- those who've never heard of it (the majority of those remaining)
- those who love it, but don't seem to really understand it (more or less all others)

The enduring tragedy of American football coverage is that while most of their pundits and commentators belong to the fourth category (e.g. famous ESPN 'color-announcer' Ty Keough, who at least has a bona fide history in the game), a goodly proportion of them show alarming signs of belonging to the first. There is a highly credible body of opinion out there that commentator Jack Edwards, to name but one, is merely biding his time announcing for the Major League of Sawker in the secret hope of eventually transferring over to big-time gridiron football coverage.

In a country where ice hockey is, and will remain, a

bigger sport than association football, one has to expect a rather skewed view of the universal game. And, thankfully, that's what they give us. Those Yanks are prolific generators of footballing ludicrousness, and long may they continue to be. Where would we be without them? Hail to the Guff.

THE ALSO-RANS

☆John O'Brien
In a nutshell: Ajax and Team USA stalwart.
Gaffta Panel Verdict: Guff not a priority as actually quite good at football.

'I saw a bunch of heads, and the Mohawk was open. I was trying to hit the Mohawk.'

☆Alexi Lalas
In a nutshell: Bearded centre-half-cum-troubadour at heart of US defence in 1994 World Cup.
Gaffta Panel Verdict: If there was a musical award, he'd give Gazza and Hod a run for their money.

'Anywhere I've played, I've been tested and understood what's been banned. Random testing isn't so random when you're a long-haired freak.'

☆Bruce Arena
In a nutshell: America's answer to Alex Ferguson.
Gaffta Panel Verdict: Can't quite add a Gaffta to his MLS titles.

'But give our guys credit, they never gave up. They were running around like a bunch of idiots, but they never quit. Idiots with heart.'

☆John Dykes

In a nutshell: Cable commentator responsible for a memorable assessment of Wayne Rooney's famous winner for Everton against Arsenal.

Gaffta Panel Verdict: Needs to emulate Rooney and show this kind of form on the international stage.

'It must be a young man that tries to lob Seaman twice in two minutes.'

THE NOMINEES

☆Ty Keough

In a nutshell: Little-loved yet 'proper' USA soccer man.

Gaffta Panel Verdict: Almost European in his guff-ness.

Ty Keough is firmly established as a 'color' commentator for ABC Sports and ESPN soccer coverage in the USA. He's not without a credible footballing pedigree, being the son of Harry Keough, star of the World Cup 1950 US team that defeated England, and having himself represented the US at the Olympics and in World Cup matches, playing, according to an ABC Sports blurb, 'on some of the most hallowed grounds of world soccer, including . . . Lansdowne Road'. He also played indoor soccer professionally with the unfortunately named St Louis Steamers and has a host of official coaching badges.

None of this has done much to prevent him from irritating a great many people in his capacity as sports broadcaster. His body language has been likened to that of 1980s cybernetic celebrity Max Headroom; his voice has been described rather succinctly as 'annoying'. His principal commentating trademark is a compulsion to fill all dead air with bizarre chatter.

'The ball is an optical illusion as it's painted asymmetrically.'
Pity Ty isn't an illusion.

'The ball was actually picking up speed as it approached the goal!'
Reminds one of the classic Big Ron remark about the shot that was 'rising and dipping at the same time'.

'He's got those greenish-yellowish shoes on, so he looks fast.'
If he played for Norwich, he'd look even faster.

'I was expecting one of those Claudio Reyna through-passes that no one expects.'
A case of being more El Tel than the El Tels themselves?

'It can be difficult to score if the ball is in your half.'
Ditto.

'Donovan goes nutmeg!'
Only in America . . .

'For the US, disappointment because they knew this was coming.'
If they had known they'd lose, they wouldn't have been disappointed at all.

At a match where Scot Hugh Dallas officiated:
'Reyna appears to have gotten off scot-free . . . no pun intended.'
No pun made, either.

'Cannavaro the meat-eater!'
Pun successfully made here. But regrettably so.

'Del Piero always wears the captain's armband with the C upside down so he can read it when he's celebrating.'
Is it C for 'captain' or C for 'celebrate'?

'Dude, I think you're gettin' a card.'
American version of George Hamilton's famous tongue-lashing for Lilian Laslandes, 'You, sir, are an idiot!'

Famously, Ty has a marked propensity towards getting key facts wrong:
'They call him the Mad Hungarian.'
About Bulgarian striker Hristo Stoichkov.

'I wouldn't be surprised if European teams try to sign him [Paraguayan Miguel Benitez].'
Benitez played for Espanol de Barcelona at the time.

But Ty's backroom staff aren't any better. Surely Ty is fatally undermined when a caption runs across the bottom of the screen during a match saying:
'Del Piero is one of the best players in Syria'.
'Serie A' sounds a bit like 'Syria', but still . . .

Another Ty trait that gets the back of many a viewer up is his rather questionable football analysis:
'Valderrama is arguably the best midfielder in the world.'
The fact that semi-retired Valderrama was arguably not even the best midfielder at Tampa Bay Mutiny need not detain us here.

'The violence that erupted in Marseilles could have been avoided if England had played earlier, so its followers would have had a game to occupy them to help them blow off some of their pent-up energy. By scheduling the

match so late, it allowed boredom to settle in – almost coaxing them into starting and/or looking for trouble. They needed to pour their emotions into a meaningful early match rather than into the streets of Marseilles.'

Ty probes deep into the psyche of the typical English football yob.

But Ty does have his moments. He has a nice double act going with perennial commentary partner (and brother-in-viewer-irritation) Jack Edwards.

Ty: Sicily has an active volcano, actually named Mt Arena.
Edwards: Bruce has had an eruption or two.
Ty: And a rumbling of the earth!
Edwards: And some release of steam! But you don't want to get caught in those steam vents!

Later in the same match . . .

Ty: Is that some rumbling and steam coming from Mt Arena?
Edwards: Yes some seismic activity definitely – I believe that was a Sicilian word with no English translation.

In another match:

Ty: When you meet Iuliano and Tomassi, check your insurance policies!
Edwards: And your life and health policies!
Ty: And wear your shinguards front and back!

Back-shinguards? Ty should get in there with a patent before Craig Johnstone beats him to it.

It must be something about Ty that brings this kind of thing out of his gantry partners. Even when Jack Edwards isn't around, it still happens:

Ty: Free kick for the USA.
Rob Stone: That's a good thing, because they would hate to pay for it.

Boom and, indeed, boom.

☆ Tommy Smyth

In a nutshell: Irishman who somehow inveigled his way into American soccer coverage.

Gaffta Panel Verdict: Tommy's sense of humour doesn't always go down very well across the water.

Irishman Tommy Smyth spent the 1990s establishing himself as a fixture in ESPN Major League Soccer, Champions League, and World Cup coverage. That's not to say that he's a popular man. As a 'color commentator', he has succeeded in incurring the wrath of many a viewer. Particularly objectionable for many is his oft-used catchphrase 'onion bag', which of course is a euphemism for the goal-net (as in 'That's a pretty important bulge in the ole onion bag!'). For some reason, the most passionate Tommy-haters generally hail from New Zealand, where ESPN is available as a subscription service.

Tommy's not without a sense of humour. Every match sees him try his hand at a bit of improv:

'Leboeuf is so far up the field, he will need to call a taxi to get back in time.'

Fair enough, but Tommy doesn't know when to let it lie . . .

'Had he scored that, it would have been worth the taxi-fare.'

Always quit while you're ahead, Tommy.

'There's more contact there than in a disco in Seoul.'

What you do on your World Cup nights off is your own business, Tommy.

'Do you like your hamburgers well done? Because they will be if they don't win today.'

Inevitable quip about Hamburg SV in the Champions League.

'There's Juan Carlos, the Spanish king. So there's royalty here besides ourselves.'
This is just so wrong. Not only is Tommy the commonest of commoners, but he is not even 'here'. He's sitting behind a microphone in Connecticut watching the match on TV.

'Left-back may be Roberto Carlos's address, but you never find him at home there.'
No wonder viewers are going postal.

'Madrid don't want to go to Turin with Juventus alive.'
For bloodthirsty Tommy, football is very much a matter of life and death.

There are times you just can't argue with Tommy, no matter how much you might want to:
'Look at the German fans, they know what happened.'
Not surprising really, Tommy. Their seats are pointed towards the action.

'Liverpool don't do very well in Italy, especially against Italian teams.'
Tommy doesn't do very well in general.

'It's 1–1, and if there are no more goals it'll be a draw.'
Football's a funny old game.

Truisms are all very well, but Tommy's main stock-in-trade, as he well knows himself, is sheer out-and-out nonsense:
'He's not fast, but he's quick.'
Tommy's not crap, but he's rubbish.

'There's only three points separating the top four teams in this group.'
The group is, of course, a Champions League group of four.

'The ball is turning away, but if it turns itself in, it's in the back of the net.'
Hope it's one of those self-steering footballs, then.

'He deserved the free kick but was fortunate to get it.'
Tommy's fortunate to be a commentator, but deserves something else.

'If you drew a line that the lawnmower has drawn, then you'd see he wasn't offside.'
All linesmen should be equipped with lawnmowers.

'Kelly knows all about Luis Enrique because he played against him for the Republic of Ireland against Portugal recently.'
Luis Enrique is, of course, Spanish.

'I'd say he's got a chance of selling shoes.'
Tommy's baffling response when asked about Arrigo Saachi's chances of being the next England manager.

'Nedved really hasn't done very little in the midfield.'
Not a little praise from Tommy.

'Vennegoor just turns and lampoons it into the net.'
He unveils satire as PSV's secret striking weapon.

'It must be hard to convince yourself you're playing on the road when you're playing at home.'
Must be even harder to think of a reason to do so.

'The [offside] rule was done perfectly, but I still don't agree with it.'
There's no pleasing Tommy.

'Synergy. I love that word, don't you? Sometimes you keep the good wine till last.'
Need a dictionary, sir?

☆Ray Hudson

In a nutshell: Geordie gaffer with a nasty streak plying his trade in Major League Sawker.

Gaffta Panel Verdict: Sack from DC United gig put halt to guff gallop.

Little Freddy Adu might be grabbing all the headlines Stateside, but it's his ex-gaffer at DC United that's carving quite a name for himself in the guff stakes. Hudson, like approximately 37 per cent of leading guffsters, is actually a Geordie. He famously tried to bring Gazza to Washington a few years back.

A recurring problem for Ray at United was the less than clinical finishing from his strikers. Happily, however, in times of desperation came inspiration . . . for guff:

'We don't have a ruthless streak. We're like Dracula looking at a beautiful neck. We don't have the fangs to sink in.'

'I just want to vomit now. It was finger-down-the-throat finishing.'

'Without penetration, it's just masturbation, and right now, we're playing with ourselves.'

'This isn't a scientific thing – sometimes you just need a little luck. Unfortunately, Lady Luck keeps showing us her big, ugly ass.'

Of course Ray's stint in the capital wasn't without its moments. The arrival of Freddy cheered him up for a while:

'A blind man galloping on a horse can see his talent.'

And fellow striker Dema Kovalenko mightn't have been the most assured in front of goal, but if you wanted someone to perform a random act of savage violence . . .

'He is a footballer. He's got great feet. He's a good link man, a great outlet. He challenges. He would stab his grandmother in the eye for another bowl of porridge.'

Keeper Nick Rimando can go all the way. Well, some of the way anyhow:
'That was a world-class save. That is the kind of thing that gives you the belief that Nicky is a pure 14-carat star.'

And youngster Eliseo Quintanilla seems to be maturing nicely:
'He's starting to grow some hair on his balls.'

Ray is not a man to be messed with. In his previous gig in charge of the Miami Fusion, he was less than impressed with the first-team squad he inherited:
'A flea-ridden dog without a lick of respect.'

And at United even Hristo Stoichkov, the crankiest man in world football, finally met his match, pulling one strop too many after getting the curly finger and earning Hudson the kudos of weary coaches from Bulgaria to Barcelona:
'Sit down and shut the f**k up!'

Rather more worryingly, the ability to wield a knife with a view to causing maximum damage does seem inordinately important to Ray. After a 'clutch road win', he roared:
'We stabbed 'em right in the heart, and it was beautiful.'

WINNER

☆ Jack Edwards

In a nutshell: US sports broadcaster in the traditional mould slumming it in the Major League of Sawker.

Gaffta Panel Verdict: This man is one of the founding fathers of the Land of the Free, the Home of the Guff.

Jack Edwards is a leading 'play-by-play man' for ABC Sports and ESPN (usually partnered by fellow Gaffta nominee Ty Keough). An Emmy Award-winning all-rounder who likes to pepper his soccer commentary with ice-hockey terminology and lashings of bias and jingoism, Jack has covered just about every sport under the sun, including sumo, Little League baseball, gymnastics, golf and ski-jumping. One gets the impression that he's serving time as a soccer 'announcer' in the hope that it leads to bigger and better things.

That's not to say that matches don't affect him. He got famously emotional during the USA's overachieving blaze of glory through the 2002 World Cup.

In their opening match, the USA faced mighty Portugal. Few gave them any hope of even a draw. Little wonder, then, that when the USA found themselves 3–0 up, Jack reckoned:
'This is stunning people all over Europe.'

And then, just to rub it in:
'This is stopping traffic all over Europe.'

Then, perhaps with a weather-eye on twentieth-century history, he remarked that:
'Korean fans are not happy.'

The Portuguese pulled one back, but this didn't faze Jack:
'Wake up your friends! It's US leading Portugal, 3–1.'

It went to 3–2, but the Americans survived. Jack was beside himself. It was all Old Glory, the Spirit of 1776 and the Battle Hymn of the Republic:

'Mine eyes have seen the glory! The US has shocked Portugal.'

He was equally agog as the USA fought a valiant rearguard action against the South Koreans. Particular praise went to keeper Brad Friedel, who played a blinder:

'Brad Friedel is from Mars – he's certainly not of this planet!'

Certain other goalkeepers are probably from Venus:

'Kasey Keller, eat your heart out!'

He could even wring some excitement out of the USA's 3–1 defeat at the hands of the moribund Poles:

'This is huge! This is a winner-go-home, loser-go-on situation!'

He almost had to be sedated when the USA defeated Mexico in the second round:

'The Land of the Free, the Home of the Brave are through to the quarter-finals of the World Cup!'

During more humdrum matches, such as Turkey v. Brazil, he could afford to be a bit more cavalier:

'Look at that little Basturk run.'

Jack has a whole host of catchphrases that together comprise what may in time develop into a fully fledged dialect to rival Big Ron's Ronglish. Let's have a look at some of its major components:

CLIMBING THE LADDER:
Heading the ball. So, for example, a miscued header triggers the remark:
'He couldn't climb the ladder fast enough.'
Variations on the theme may occur occasionally:
'Neuville couldn't get on the last rung there.'

LAWNMOWER MOVE:
Hacking someone down. As in:
'That's a good lawnmower move, actually. If the grass is kinda long, you do that a few times.'

SPEED MOVE:
Any piece of action involving running (i.e. almost all action).

THREADING THE NEEDLE:
Dribbling past a couple of defenders.

PK REJECTION:
Keeper saves a penalty.

HEAD GAIN:
Defensive header, thankfully ladder-free.

INFIELD ATTRITIONAL:
A tackle.

But don't let the above fool you into thinking that Jack is some sort of master of the spoken word:
'Thuram has torn his shirt and it's a two-layered affair. You can see the blue underneath . . . actually that's flesh.'
Maybe it was a very cold day.

'Part of the US philosophy tonight has to be that if the ball is actually flying through the air for 75 minutes, they only have to defend for 15.'
Talk about low expectations.

'Nobody's even dripping wet because of the precipitation.'
Jack lambastes the USA for a lack of commitment so profound that it even stops the rain from touching them.

'With Italy, it's like shooting a bullet through a forest – one of the bullets will hit a tree before it gets to the clearing.'
Jack explains how playing the Italians is akin to a botched murder attempt.

'It's yellow-card-a-go-go!!'
Careful, Jack – you might give some ESPN executive an idea for a horrific prime-time extravaganza.

'His eyes were as big as pie plates when he saw the goal.'
But his eyes were bigger than his belly because he missed the chance.

'As any coach will tell you, a team with a two-goal advantage has the worst-possible half-time lead.'
It's the first question of the Grade 1 FIFA coaching badge exam.

'The new ball is a rocket without tail feathers.'
Sounds like close control is going to be a bit difficult.

'Beckham makes a perfect pass into the trash can.'
A case of giving credit where it's not due?

'Albright hits the post! That's Chris Albright at his best!'
Jack damns with faint praise.

'That's a slide tackle just like they teach you at soccer camp!'
Jack accidentally reveals ESPN's major soccer audience.

'Claudio Reyna provides maximum optimal options for the United States.'
The first thing they teach you at soccer camp is to provide maximum optimal options.

'The Brazilians have golf clubs for feet.'
Jack gets to the bottom of Brazilian football mastery.

'Materazzi says, "You go down too easy, bitch, be a man!"'
Jack's not happy with Claudio Reyna's lack of resilience in the face of a 'lawnmower move'.

THE JOHNNY FOREIGNER AWARD

10. **'A derby is a derby . . . and vice versa.'**
Mario Jardel on a clash between Benfica and Sporting Lisbon

9. **'Sometimes in football you have to score goals.'**
Thierry Henry

8. **'Football is simple, you're either on time, or you're too late. If you're too late, then you have to leave earlier.'**
That great philosopher, Johan Cruyff

7. **'I don't really like the north. It's always raining, it's very cold and I don't like all those little houses.'**
Frédéric Kanouté doesn't fancy a move to Blackburn

6. **'Someone said to me, "You Italian f***ing b*******." I know I am Italian, they do not have to tell me.'**
Paolo Di Canio

5. **'The best Manchester United player is Michael Owen.'**
Pelé

4. **'My goals in Holland were known as 'stiffies', which means something quite different in England, of course.'**
Dennis Bergkamp

3. **Journalist: After watching you run today, it makes me wonder how many lungs you have.**
Ren Houseman: Well, you know, I have one, like everybody else.'

2. **'I am happy when our fans are happy, when our players**

are happy and our chairman is on the moon.'
Claudio Ranieri

1. **'At a certain point in this match we were at the edge of the abyss . . . but we did the right thing, kept calm and so we were able to take the step forward.'**
Portuguese international, João Pinto

THE
GAFFTA
AWARDS

THE GREEN GUFF AWARD

It's all very well castigating the UK's pantheon of nonsense-merchants, but deserving of our opprobrium though they are, they are not the only ones. One only has to take a short ferry ride westwards from Liverpool to wind up in another English-speaking hotbed of football-related foolishness – the island of Ireland. It's a fact that the Irish produce more hot air per head than any other nation on earth. Little wonder the Gaffta committee has seen fit to give them an award of their own!

Some would argue that of all the TV channels on these islands, RTE does football coverage the best. With John Giles, Eamon Dunphy and Liam Brady as pundits, and able anchor Bill O'Herlihy officiating over proceedings, one often has a source of interesting and coherent argument about the modern game. But more importantly, one also has a rich source of comedy, both intentional and entirely accidental. Between O'Herlihy's mischievously leading questions, Giles's bizarre mix of wisdom and lack of interest in extraneous details (such as players' names), Dunphy's firebrand rants and Brady's curmudgeonliness, the classic moments come thick and fast.

Then there are the commentators. George Hamilton could, and does, mix metaphors for Ireland. His opposite number on TV3, Big Trev Welch, would give Clive a run for his money down the Man United superstore. And then there's the ancient, venerable Jimmy Magee, whose 'pigeons of peace' quote has spanned the globe.

Thanks to these individuals, the small island of Ireland remains one of the world's prime exporters of guff to this very day.

THE ALSO-RANS

☆Noel King

In a nutshell: Squat League of Ireland toiler and managerial merry-go-round passenger who loves being on the telly.

Gaffta Panel Verdict: Mirroring his career on the park, he'll never cross the water to play with the big boys.

'Lovely little simple intricate passes.'

'He's gone too erect, no shape at all there, and there she goes.'

☆Trevor Welch

In a nutshell: Bulky, Man U-obsessed bulwark of Irish TV3's sports coverage.

Gaffta Panel Verdict: Comic moments abound, but seldom transfer onto the page. Expect great things from Trev in future.

'Juventus are waiting to remodelise the stadium, John.'

'Celtic have an Old Firm derby game coming up this weekend . . . against Rangers.'

'And Celtic have extended their lead at the top to a remarkable 15 points. Now to soccer . . .'

'Australia have failed narrowly to miss out on all of the major competitions.'

☆Roddy Collins

In a nutshell: Classic Dublin wide boy made good.
Gaffta Panel Verdict: Roddy's nothing if not a talker, so his future looks bright.

An ambitious man, the ex-Carlisle manager:
'**Everything I do in club football will just be part of my apprenticeship until I get the Ireland job.**'

Including this, Roddy?
'**I thought John McCarthy was having an absolute stinker. It was only when I was going to take him off that I was told he had been sent off five minutes earlier.**'

'**United go home having given one of the top Division Two sides a much more difficult day than most plaudits expected.**'

☆Jackie Fullerton

In a nutshell: Soporific describer of Northern Ireland's international travails.
Gaffta Panel Verdict: The guff is there to be heard if you can stay awake long enough.

'**The Spanish fans are encouraging their players to get forward, and the Northern Ireland fans are also encouraging their players.**'

After Spain went 3–0 up:
'**Northern Ireland haven't been embarrassed, and that's the main thing.**'

'**We've got a moth back in our commentary box . . . here's Vicente . . . Gerry has caught the moth, just as Vicente was trying to sting like a butterfly . . . no, a bee, of course.**'

☆Kevin Moran

In a nutshell: Great player in his day. Should have slipped out of the public eye while the going was good.

Gaffta Panel Verdict: Impressive guffster by dint of utter lack of information content in what he says.

Packie Bonner: It's crucial to get an away goal, isn't it, Kevin?

Kevin Moran: Yes, the away team always want to get an away goal, and at the same time, the home team like to keep a clean sheet, know what I mean?

Packie Bonner: What about Milan? Can they win it, Kevin?

Kevin Moran: They're one of the teams, any of the teams really. The teams tomorrow night as well. They're all the best teams in the Champions League really, know what I mean?

Packie Bonner: I like Juventus, Kevin. What do you think?

Kevin Moran: They're strong, they're doing well, know what I mean?

Packie Bonner: Ajax have some fantastic players, Kevin.

Kevin Moran: Yeah, I like the lad van der Fart and little Pienaard is quick, very quick feeted.

This time Kevin, no, we don't know what you mean.

☆Stephen Alkin

In a nutshell: Middle-aged commentating understudy at Ireland's RTE.

Gaffta Panel Verdict: Lack of airtime hinders guff production.

'The Stamford Bridge crowd was doing its own impersonation of . . . silence.'

'Well, he almost touched the paper there.'

'Chalk and cheese, that's Carlo Cudicini. And that was the cheese.'

☆Darragh Moloney

In a nutshell: RTE's second-choice football commentator rarely utters a word out of turn. More's the pity.

Gaffta Panel Verdict: Little guff to extract from this one's commentary. Needs to try harder.

'Let's see what RTE Sport has in the way of sport this week.'
No, let's see what they have in the way of fine cuisine.

'St Mary's cost £32,000 to build, and today it's filled to its 32,000 capacity.'

'The Koreans are trying to score here.'
Unveiling a brand new tactic.

THE NOMINEES

☆Eamon Dunphy

In a nutshell: Acerbic journalist/broadcaster/former player famed for courting controversy.

Gaffta Panel Verdict: Age may have mellowed Eamo. These days, it seems like he actually aims for guff.

Most will know Dunphy as the apparent ghostwriter-with-artistic-licence who gallantly attempted to rescue Roy Keane from the FA by suggesting he'd actually made up all those terrible things about Alf-Inge Haaland in Roy's book.

However, in his other life as a football pundit, the ex-Millwall man has become by far Ireland's most prolific source of natural gas. Dunphy has risked life and limb slating successive Irish gaffers, much to the chagrin of Ireland's 'Greatest Fans in the World™'. He wore Cameroon colours in the studio during Ireland's World Cup 2002 kick-off in protest at the treatment of his hero and muse, and followed in Keano's footsteps later in the tournament by being sent home in disgrace by RTE for being 'tired and emotional' on-air.

Eamo's favoured guff technique involves picking an Irish national team manager, chucking a biro across a studio and roaring a random selection of the following adjectives: congenital loser, sham, embarrassment, scurvy pup, wagon, spoofer, decentskin, imposter, bully.

THE DUNPHY GUFFBANK:

'The overwhelming view of the listeners is that . . . they are split down the middle.'
Talkshow host Eamo begins another Keane defence excitedly before realising the numbers aren't quite with him.

'When you weed out the nutters, it's around 80–20 behind Roy.'
Not to be deterred, Eamo the Democrat finds a way.

'Usually it takes a bottle of Bacardi and a gallon of Coke to get John out of his seat.'
Eamo bemused by Johnny Gilesy good-humour shocker after Ireland score.

Giles: Football fans have short memories, Eamon.
Dunphy: I found at Millwall that fans had long memories, John. They never forgot how bad I was! HA HA HA HA HA!
Giles: [Silence]

Bill: [on Sam Allardyce's survival as Bolton manager] They'll be dancing on the streets of Limerick.
Eamo: They'll be dancing on the streets of Limerick anyway, Bill.

'These aren't the incidents that win and lose games. These are false.'
Eamo's tired-and-emotional view of the two Russian goals that won their World Cup clash with Tunisia.

'He's one of the biggest whingers in world football . . . he's a bloody eejit.'
Probably the nicest thing he's ever said about Mick McCarthy.

'History is today and tomorrow.'
Furious Eamo goes on the defensive after Billo questions Keane's 'legacy'.

'Eamon Dunphy is a nobody with one virtue: honesty and realism.'
Eamo pays a mathematically imprecise tribute to himself.

'The first two-syllable word I learned when I was growing up was "discretion".'
Numbers just aren't his thing, are they?

'Kilbane's head is better than his feet. If only he had three heads, one on the end of each leg.'

☆John Giles

In a nutshell: Former legend on the field now elder statesman of punditry.
Gaffta Panel Verdict: With the passing of the years, Gilesy gets better and better.

John Giles is a former Leeds and Ireland hatchet man nowadays turned grand old gent of Irish punditry. He's also the brother-in-law of Nobby Stiles:
'My sister Kay's never forgiven me. Nobby's no oil painting, is he?'
Gilesy has seen it all, and is rightly suspicious of modern

players. He remembers all too well the bad old days of under-achieving Ireland and tells of a 4–0 reverse in Budapest after which one of the five-man FAI selection committee popped his head round the dressing-room door. 'Fantastic, lads! Best performance I've ever seen from an Irish side.' It took Gilesy a few seconds to work it out – Hungary had worn green that day. 'For f★★★'s sake, Pat, we were wearing our change strip!'

Most of Gilesy's commentary is devoted to eulogising players with the 'moral courage' to 'put their foot on the ball' and knock a few 'bread-and-butter passes'. Also a strong believer that national stereotyping beats research any day of the week. Italians will always defend well, Africans will be 'a little bit naive, Bill' and East Europeans 'probably won't fancy it', particularly their goalkeepers.

The key to most of Gilesy's guff triumphs is his unintentional Laurel and Hardy relationship with RTE anchor, Bill O'Herlihy. This double act has got it all . . .

INSIGHT:

Billo: This [UEFA Cup final] is something of a local derby between Holland and Germany.
Gilesy: Er . . . yeah, they've been close to each other for years . . .

WILDEAN IMPROVISATION:

Billo: We'll draw the winners out of a hat a little later in the programme.
Gilesy: [Rare moment of frivolity] A top hat, Bill?
Billo: [Quick as you like] Yes, a top hat, John. We got it out of your wardrobe.

GRITTY REALISM:

Billo: [Pre-World Cup] Sixteen days from now we'll all walk a little taller, won't we, John?
Gilesy: Well, er, I don't think we'll be any taller, Bill.

LIVELY BANTER:
Billo: What are you actually saying, John?
Gilesy: What am I saying?
Billo: Yeah.
Gilesy: I would be more confident that we could win this game now than before the game.
Billo: You could be a cock-eyed optimist.
Gilesy: I'm not.

Gilesy: It's like the old George Formby song 'Waiting on the Corner'.
Billo: 'Leaning on the Lamppost', you mean?
Gilesy: Yeah.
Billo: Are you going to sing it?
Gilesy: No.

Billo: We've a big game tomorrow night. And of course it's a big game for us as well.
Giles: [Grinning] Yeah, let's hope everyone is watching.
Billo: You're very sarcastic tonight, John.
Giles: I'm not being sarcastic, Bill. It's ahhhh very important. Ahhhh. Ratings. Ahh.
Billo: That's right, John.

THE BEST UNINTENTIONAL GAGS IN TOWN:
Billo: Carsley lacks a bit of skill in those situations. Let's call a spade a spade.
Gilesy: Yes, Bill, he's in there to dig.

THE REST OF GILESY'S GUFFBANK:
On the big match atmosphere:
'I'd rather play in front of a full house than an empty crowd.'

On Spurs' fallen saviour:
'Hoddle's career in management has been a bit of a mixed grill.'

On Danny Mills:
'He's a stupid footballer who does stupid things.'

Concerned that holding interviews for the Irish manager's job discriminated against less eloquent candidates:
'Interviews is a nonsense.'

Defending forwards who go down easily:
'It's like somebody walking down the street and there's a big block of wood. If you don't see it, you're going to walk into it and fall over.'

What it's all about?
'A good manager will make 11 players look like a good team, whereas a bad manager will make 11 players look like a bad team.'

On Robbie Keane's inability to tackle tricky long reds off the top cushion:
'The difference between him playing and Ken Doherty, though he is a big stout-hearted lad, is huge.'
The player's name is Gary Doherty, Gilesy.

And on the declining standards in world football:
'The problem is, Bill, that the kids nowadays have got personal stereos and higher education.'

☆ Damien Richardson

In a nutshell: League of Ireland personage not made good.
Gaffta Panel Verdict: By rights should be nowhere near the guff big leagues, but the sheer verbal audacity of the man gets him a nod.

Damien 'Rico' Richardson is one of the true literary giants of our time, a master wordsmith who bridges the gap between the equally rarefied worlds of world-class football and world-class literature.

No, not really, but he'd like to be. That's the tragedy of it, really, because Rico's ugly scuffles with the English language – both as a football 'analyst' on Irish TV3's *Sports Tonight* and in print – will reduce you to tears for all the wrong reasons. When Rico opens his gob or puts pen to paper, overly ambitious, ludicrously ornate sentences crash about him like the walls of a house built without foundations.

Rico's stock-in-trade, if he only knew it, is the befuddlement of the common man. Sentences beginning with the word 'whether' are a particular danger. Here, Rico looks to the future:

'Whether one is blessed with a prodigious flair for articulacy or merely entrusted with a basic monosyllabic uttering of contentment, the relevance of this coming season will stimulate in every green and white heart at least a temporary escalation in embellished eloquence, so as to allow all an opportunity to express the most wondrous sense of anticipation and excitement that lies within.'

He can be philosophical when his team loses the top spot in the league – too philosophical for his own good. Again, note the daredevil use of the word 'whether':

'Whether one possesses the stoical stature of an empirical philosopher or a more mundane propensity for self-gratification, the cataclysmic effect of one's removal from pole position in the most senior league in the country could be most injurious.'

Carelessly, he reveals who taught him English in his youth, thereby putting them in danger of revenge attacks by traumatised readers:

'If the remnants of my classical education at the sometimes not-so tender hands of the Christian Brothers of Donore Avenue and Drimnagh Castle serve me correctly, it was that Greek playmaker of old, Epicurus,

who stated that "the misfortune of the wise is better than the prosperity of the fool".'

How Rico prospers these days. He's got a car, you know:
'The last miles home on a long journey appear unending at the best of times, but traffic congestion when in sight of the homeland only serves to test further the resolve of those concerned.'

Not that he's any better at maths:
'Seven draws is an awful lot. If Bohs had won two or three of those and even lost the rest, they'd be in a wonderful position.'

Particularly troubling is Rico's desire to speak the same way he writes – whatever vestige of editing he applies to his writing is of course completely absent from his TV punditry. Below is a mere taste of Rico's oral crimes against the English language:
'I felt there was a lack of definable objectivity about both teams.'

'This is the last and final goal from the Turks.'

'The Russians will be big and strong if you let them be big and strong.'

'Maldini has really regurgitated his career at left-back.'

'There was a lack of interdepartmental choreography between midfield and attack.'

'Brian, I know you've got your backbone set in stone.'

'The Waterford player's shot was on target, which is an important aspect of a player's shot.'

☆Frank Stapleton

In a nutshell: Dour former Ireland striker now plying his trade on lesser-watched Sky Sports broadcasts.

Gaffta Panel Verdict: Guff strike rate at least as impressive as his strike rate in front of goal during his heyday.

It's hard to believe that not so long ago Stapo was an enthusiastic, lively frontman in high demand among the powerhouses of European football. Jimmy Hill once remarked of Frank the player:

'Manchester United are looking to Stapleton to pull some magic out of the fire.'

That would have been a neat trick. Nowadays, however, there's precious little magic, and even less fire, on offer from Frank the pundit. In fact, Frank is undoubtedly the glummest man on TV – perhaps even the glummest man in Europe – continually living down to Big Ron's famous remark:

'He smiles in the mirror first thing every morning – just to get it over with.'

If you had to choose a commentator for your funeral, it would likely be Frank. You wouldn't want Gray and Tyler hyping the thing up, and you could imagine Frank catching the mood nicely as they lowered the coffin. Peculiarly, however, Stapo's hangdog demeanour and less-than-sparkling repartee haven't prevented him from carving quite a niche for himself in the punditry game.

Moreover, conspiracy theorists consider it no coincidence that Frank's prominence on Sky Sports and TV3 has coincided with the decline of the British sitcom. Let's face it, why bother writing comedy when Frank can effortlessly create an Albert-Steptoe-meets-Manuel-from-Barcelona character for a fraction of the cost.

Though the humour may be entirely unintentional, when Frank's in the studio there's no need for canned laughter.

Of the mysteries held by a spherical object:
'You've got to be careful. You're not sure if the ball is going to bounce up or down.'

On the maddening inconsistency of some referees:
'He didn't get booked for the yellow card.'

On the complex bone alignment of the foreign player:
'He's got a knock on his shin there, just above the knee.'

Sharing his optimistic views on the evaporation of surface water:
'Once the players start running on it, it'll disappear.'

Playing up the Manuel angle:
'We have to remember Damien Duff is one of the most good players in the Premiership.'

And displaying a slight misunderstanding of the term 'rabbit punch':
'I think he's caught him. It was like a punch you'd get off your rabbit.'

To be fair to Frank, he's never truly that wide of the mark, and perhaps it's his very proximity to the right word or phrase that makes it all the funnier when he opts for the wrong one.

Why was that a free kick, Frank?
'Well, his foot was high and that's why he got his penalism.'

We hear Liverpool need a few quid. Maybe they should charge their players a subscription:
'Liverpool could do with an outlay from their wide players.'

'West Ham have weathered the storm, although it was really only a tempest.'
Meteorology never a strong point, eh?

Even when Frank is technically spot on – there's still always something quite not right:

'1–1 is probably a fair reflection of the score at half-time.'
Well, it's a decent guess anyway.

'Because of the lack of noise, you thought United had scored again because when they have scored, that's all we've heard.'
Wish we couldn't hear you, Frank.

'If either side was to draw tonight, they'd still be favourites to get through.'
Funnily enough, both sides drew. What a coincidence.

Sadly, his ability to craft cutting-edge live comedy isn't always enough to keep Frank interested. On his regular Champions League gig on TV3, commentator Trevor Welch has been forced to invest in a high-voltage cattle prod to ensure Frank doesn't nod off and tumble out of the gantry.

Welch: Has he handled the match well, Graham Poll?
Frank: [Silence]
Welch: It's been a difficult match to handle. Hasn't it, Frank?
Frank: [Silence]
Welch: Frank?
Welch: They've handled Kluivert well, haven't they, Frank?
Frank: [Silence]
Welch: Kluivert has been quiet, hasn't he?
Frank: [Silence]
Welch: Frank?

In fairness, when Frank does wake up, there's no finer computational mind in football. Particularly impressive was a marvellous on-the-spot damage assessment when Switzerland's Johann Vogel was sent off during Euro 2004:
'Their chances of winning are diminished by . . . [an ever so

slight pause as Frank's finely tuned brain performs some complex calculations] . . . 30 per cent.'

☆ Jimmy Magee

In a nutshell: Once the main man of Irish sports commentary, now fallen back into the peloton.

Gaffta Panel Verdict: Jimmy's unique logic and sentence construction will always make him a guff big-hitter.

The era when Irishman Jimmy Magee almost single-handedly provided RTE commentary for every major sporting event on earth (e.g. World Cup, Olympics, Tour de France, Cassius Clay/Muhammad Ali fights) has long gone. Nowadays, George Hamilton is RTE Commentator Numero Uno, and a host of minor characters feed on the crumbs discarded by George.

But Jimmy has enjoyed something of a renaissance in the last few years, and now plays a prominent role in RTE's Premiership coverage. His unique commentary style, once dismissed as being obtrusively gauche, has in latter days gained deserved recognition for being . . . well, not as obtrusively gauche as once thought. Indeed, 'Essence of Jimmy' is a spice that can bring life to the most humdrum of mid-table Premiership encounters.

Big fan of the pun is Jimmy . . .

'Lee must attempt to keep Cech, the Czech, in check.'

'Brennan, blocking Blockhin out of the game.'

'Fowler, living up to his name.'

He also likes to make a pithy quip when circumstances allow:

'With the goal empty, Nicky Butt, if he can manage it, should kick himself.'

Butt misses a sitter, but Magee finishes clinically.

'Peter "Superglue" Rufai!'
High praise from Jimmy for the Nigerian keeper.

'He's marking him so close, he'll probably go into the dressing-room with him at half-time.'
Jimmy revives a hoary old football cliché.

'He could sell advertising on the soles of his boots.'
And again.

'Jay Jay Okocha, so good they named him twice.'
Peter Drury thought of it first, but still . . .

'Demyanenko – he's earned his roubles tonight!'
Given Soviet communism's egalitarian approach to salaries, does this mean he played no better than anyone else?

'It's five years in Siberia for that man.'
Jimmy's ill-advised remark about a bit of slapdash USSR defending that reputedly prompted a demand for an apology from the Soviet embassy.

Perhaps inspired by the example of Big Ron's dialect Ronglish, in recent years Jimmy has begun construction of his very own nascent lingo, which we like to call 'Jimmy Mageese'. Hope it catches on . . .
'Is that a bring-down?'

'He got a two-fist to it.'

'Great ball-kill by Given.'

'Strong volleyball hand from Sorensen.'

'Nothing forthcoming in the land of the penalty.'

'Oh, shady goalkeeping!'

'A lay-on for Rep . . .'
Presumably the opposite of a lay-off.

'A little bit of the stagework from Muller.'
Muller goes down like Buddy Holly. Jimmy's not impressed.

'A crackeroo from Pete Beardsley!!'
The 'Pete' bit is especially genius.

'Givens claiming a sandwich . . .'
Not a good idea to start a match on an empty stomach.

But academic Jimmy's not just a languages man. He's also a master of maths. He's developed a useful algebraic formula to help referees figure out when a player needs to be sent off:
'Y + Y = Red.'

He'd probably be loath to admit it, but Jimmy's also a dab hand at the risqué 'Ooh, Matron'-style comment:
'Ardiles strokes the ball like it was part of his anatomy.'

'Tigana has spent the entire half inside Liam Brady's shorts.'

Jimmy's a dedicated, even obsessive, fan of all sorts of sport. That doesn't stop his match analysis from sometimes being a little bit off . . .
'Can Ormerod finish? He can, but the wrong side of the goalframe.'

'They said it was the group of death. In the end it was very much the group of survival, particularly for those who survived.'

'So much tension in football, even for these people who don't have to play.'

'If Ireland had scored more goals, they would have won the match.'

'Ha, ha, ha! He headed it away! How about that! He likes to be called a character, and he's earned it now on the televisions of the world!'

Jimmy finds the sight of a keeper heading the ball while outside the box hilarious.

'The Argentinian Ricardo Giusti made his international debut in 1966.'

From the 1990 World Cup, here Jimmy suggests that Giusti was around four years old when he made his first appearance in an Argentina shirt.

But there's no better man than Jimmy to send in to bat during your contract negotiations:

'Wonderful save again from a goalkeeper who's been overworked and underpaid today.'

Some of his observations you just have to lump into the bizarre category:

'We've got a lot of meat ahead of us between now and six o'clock!'

'And Portsmouth go off to the joyous roars of the Pompey bells.'

'Sam Allardyce with the mobile phone and the chewing gum. Which will he swallow first?'

'They're blowing bubbles again at Upton Park. Bubbles in which you may be able to read the words, "We'll be OK for next year's Premiership".'

When Jimmy gets emotional, watch out . . .

'It was great to see a united Irish side that time. Fourteen players, seven from the Republic and seven from the North played. Great days indeed. Where have all the flowers gone?'

Jimmy reminisces about an Irish eleven that once played Brazil.

'Say you find that all your heroes, Elvis Presley, Frank Sinatra, Carl Lewis, Jesse Owens, Fanny Blankers-Koen, Emile Zatopek, Enrico Caruso, Beniamino Gili and even back as far as Jesus Christ, that they were all on something, do you just cancel them all?'

Jimmy's spirited defence of sporting drugs cheats meanders into some unexpected, not to say controversial, territory.

'Horst Hrubesch from Hamburg, the Maaaan they call the Monster!'

Jimmy's legendary scream as Hrubesch steps up to take the winning penalty during the penalty shoot-out during the 1982 World Cup semi-final between Germany and France. Extensive research has failed to uncover any evidence that anyone but Jimmy has ever called Hrubesch 'the Monster'.

Thousands of semiologists worldwide are currently poring over old Jimmy commentaries, trying to get to the bottom of that unique Magee-esque sentence construction.

No, not really. But they should be. Why? Read on . . .

'Neeskens did it well on Bonhof.'

'Saw it late! Did it well!'

'Muller, who swivels his hips so well, knocks off all attackers!'

'Van Hanegem into it!'

251

'Van der Kerkhof had a real chance to write his name into those Dutch books!'

'He's blossoming today with the tempo!'

'Holzenbein has been outstandingly offensive in this World Cup!'
No need to get personal, Jimmy.

In the manner of colleague George Hamilton, sometimes Jimmy starts a sentence without being quite sure how it's going to end:
'Well, perhaps it's inflation, but the crowd are chanting that they want four. Who'd have thought they'd be thinking in that . . . high of . . . numbers.'

'Breitner has a touch of the gooooolden . . . ah . . . trophy.'

And then, of course, there's the all-time Jimmy classic, from the 1980 Olympics:
'The symbol of peace – the pigeon!'

☆Mick McCarthy
In a nutshell: Basically, the most paranoid man in football.
Gaffta Panel Verdict: Constant need to head off possible criticism makes for some remarkable utterances.

Possibly the most paranoid man in football, Mick never answers a simple question from a member of the press when an outraged defence of his record as a manager will do. On the other hand, he cuts a relaxed, almost suave figure on *Match of the Day*, where he knows they'll give him an easy time. But he wasn't always so pally with Gary Lineker. There's that little encounter in Euro '88 to consider, when Lineker rather unjustly came off the worst. Mick took away a souvenir:

'I have Gary Lineker's shirt up in my hotel room, and it's only stopped moving now.'

Of course, Mick's paranoia turned out to be more or less justified in the case of Roy Keane. Maybe it was just that Keano couldn't bear Mick's egalitarian approach to the Irish squad:
'There's no difference between Roy Keane and any other player. The only difference is he's a better player.'

'We're football people, not poets, but obviously I'm disappointed with the result.'

But he has no regrets . . . or does he?
'No regrets, none at all. My only regret is that we went out on penalties. That's my only regret. But no, no regrets.'

Despite his persecution complex, sometimes Mick has to admit that his team aren't perfect:
'It would have been hard not to be our best performance against a Premiership club since I came – because last season we were shit.'
But he still finds the excuses when it counts:
'I think one or two of our legs got a bit leg-weary.'
Medics say that's the worst kind of weariness for legs.

He had a novel, if confusing, strategy for getting into the FA Cup final:
'If we just have a final of Manchester United, us and either Tranmere or Millwall against Arsenal then we might have a chance. Scrap the semi – three versus one and we will be all right.'
Pity it didn't work out.

What Mick needs in his team are some players of this sort:
'Inter have bought the finished article and there's no doubt he can keep improving.'

'Sun Jihai pulled it back, and with Reyna they've got a nice little triangle going between them.'

Mick adds geometry to his nearly-but-not-quite list.

☆Niall Quinn

In a nutshell: Ex-Ireland beanpole striker who provides remarkably politician-like punditry.

Gaffta Panel Verdict: Desire to be all things to all men makes for some classic moments.

Depending on your taste, lanky target-man extraordinaire Quinny was either record goal-scoring Irish hero or the big lump who once got the curly finger from George Graham no more than half an hour after he'd come on as sub in the first place. Maybe it's the public's ambivalence towards his playing career that makes Quinny the pundit who wants to be, very simply, all things to all men. No public utterance passes his lips before it has been thoroughly vetted for legal, diplomatic and political correctness. In the manner of a seasoned politician, he tries to say as little as possible using as much verbiage as possible. This makes him pretty well suited to the requirements of Sky Sports, whose ideal pundit prattles away for half an hour or so while the anchor does his tax returns. Sure enough, Quinny's become an increasingly ubiquitous Sunday-afternoon presence in the high stool opposite that of Richard Keys. He's happy to field any question, so long as it doesn't require him to express an opinion that might even mildly displease someone:

'I think Arsenal will win the game, but I think Everton have a real good chance.'

If pressed, Quinny would probably opine that the ref also had a good chance of claiming all three points.

'It just shows you that Premiership football is the best in the land.'

Quinny sticks his neck out to assert that the Premiership is better than the Welsh and Scottish leagues.

'Bertie Ahern is not here catching votes today – he's here for the love of the game.'
Quinny takes a charitably non-cynical view of the Irish Prime Minister's appearance at an Ireland friendly.

But we're better off without proper Quinny opinions if this is what they'd be like:
'Roy Keane would never let his emotions destabilise the team.'
A highly non-prophetic pre-World Cup 2002 comment.

Let's be fair, though – Quinny is achingly close to being a brainy man. Every now and again he comes out with an observation that, with just a slight adjustment, would be astute, perceptive and eloquent . . .
'The little leg-over. There will be kids all over Ireland trying that tomorrow.'
Ronaldo's step-over, or 'leg-over' as Quinny has it, is yesterday's news for all and sundry, but a complete novelty for Quinny.

'Everybody has been trying to put dots on top of Ts and crosses over Is.'
But not achieving very much in the process.

'The referee should be given discretion to protect the game and protect what we're trying to achieve with football.'
Which is to have a game of football.

'He's the only referee that, when he makes a decision, there's no arms thrown into the air and no gestating.'
If it was women's football, it might be a different story.

'I'll have to see that again. In the motion of movement there, could the linesman have got that right?'
With the aid of the 'vision of seeing', he has indeed, Quinny.

'It's the sort of goal that makes the hair stand up on your shoulders.'
Hirsute Quinny has high testosterone levels, you know . . .

'With eight or ten minutes to go they were able to bring Nicky Butt back and give him fifteen to twenty minutes.'
The groundskeeper gave Butt special permission to have an extra canter around the field after the match was over.

'An incredible degree of difficulty there, but he managed to make a good hash of it in the end.'
Quinny takes some of the shine off a Jeremies volley.

'Sam Allardyce always speaks from the hips.'
Not sure what this would involve. Probably best not to ask.

'It was a stone-bonking penalty.'
Sounds a bit like an 'Ooh, Matron' type of comment, but we really don't want to think about it too much.

Speaking of which, Quinny is actually a bit of an accidental master of the double-entendre:
'Clinton likes to have his back up against the goalkeeper, to feel the defenders, and then come inside.'

'There's a danger they'll wait for that one time you expose yourself.'

'Brazil have just been touching their balls across the pitch for the last five or ten minutes.'

'He comes inside, drops the shoulder, throws the leg over, and bang.'

'The Albanians are penetrating us from all positions.'

Finally, no need to use a double entendre when a single one will do:

'Because he was reading *The Guardian*, Graeme Le Saux found his femininity being questioned.'

WINNER

☆George Hamilton
In a nutshell: Ireland's premier sports commentator.
Gaffta Panel Verdict: No point in equivocating here . . . this man is a guff genius!

When he first succeeded Jimmy Magee at the summit of the Irish commentary game, George made his mark with some self-consciously flamboyant pronunciations of foreign names. Something of a linguist by education, he became the first man on these shores to address Liverpool's rotund Danish stylist as Jan '*Molbu*'. And while lesser men baulked at his surname, George made it a lifetime's obsession to perfect the first name of Bixente Lizarazu.

While he still approaches the verbal challenges of an away tie in the Ukraine with rather too much relish, George has since introduced two more dramatic traits to his gantry handiwork: costly pre-hatch chicken counting and a fine line in outrageous metaphors.

It's to the former that the website dangerhere.com is dedicated. By our calculations, George is directly responsible for over 87 per cent of the goals the Irish national team have conceded since he first picked up a mic in Lansdowne Road. The pattern is hauntingly familiar:

'Babb and Breen have handled the threat magnificently. We're on the brink of a famous night for the boys in green . . . oh, danger here . . .'

Perhaps the most costly utterance of the dreaded 'DH' came at Euro '88 after Ronnie Whelan had shinned a bicycle kick from 30 yards to put Ireland in front against the Soviet Union. Ireland had beaten England four days earlier and the country was giddily clambering aboard the 'Jack's army' bandwagon.

Alas, George just wouldn't let it lie:

'Bonner has gone 165 minutes of these championships without conceding a goal . . .'

'Shut up, George,' roared the nation. But 'twas too late. Sure enough:

'. . . oh, danger here . . .'

Protasov did the rest and Holland finished the job the following weekend. Nobody looked further than George for the blame.

It was, unfortunately, but the tip of the iceberg. 'That should be no problem for the defence – OH NOOOO!!' is one of RTE television's most overused phrases. And then there was the Euro '92 qualifier in Poland, which saw what was – even for George – a landmark feat of fate-tempting at its most disastrous.

Ireland were 3–1 up – a majestic away performance – when George took control:

'Poland have to score twice now to draw and they will not do so.'

The Poles duly knock one in. Minutes later . . .

'I might be tempting fate but I can't see the Poles scoring . . . OH NOOOO, they just have!!'

That one took some forgiving.

George's other trademark is rather more entertaining. While he may be a man of many languages, his greatest verbal achievements have come in the mother tongue, in which his adventurous approach to metaphor construction have enlivened many a scrappy bore draw. We've already seen his magnificent 'rabbits in the headlights' classic snatch the Mixed Metaphor gong. Here are some more choice selections from George's metaphorical house of horrors.

On some rare patience from an Irish midfield:
'The midfield are like a chef . . . trying to prise open a stubborn oyster to get at the fleshy meat inside.'

Going green at Italia '90:
'The seeds of doubt that were sown against Egypt have been doused by a dose of Jack Charlton's almighty weedkiller.'

Making Ireland's Euro 2004 exit in Basel a little more tolerable:
'The flags are waving, and no doubt at the foot of the Alps, the cowbells are chiming too. And it's going to take a lot for Ireland to turn it round and sour the chocolate.'

Counting down to a Sweden–Holland penalty shootout at Euro 2004:
'It's like a train pulling into a station slowing down. There's an air of inevitability about this. It's not going to crash into the buffers. It's going to come to a gentle stop.'

Basking in the warmth of an Ireland lead:
'The eiderdown of this 2–0 lead is a lot more comfortable than the blanket of 1–0.'

Greeting Ashley Cole's last-gasp winner for Arsenal against Kiev:
'They've really eked this one out. Like coal miners mining their seam until they finally reach the surface with their precious black gold.'

Porto's third in the Champions League final produces an unlikely reference to a famous Dublin meeting point:

'And Flavio Roma was left there like a jilted lover under Clery's Clock.'

A diminutive but versatile fellow, George is not just a man for the set pieces. On the contrary, his all-round approach to guff creation has marked him out as the Johann Cruyff of the gantry – a total guff merchant.

Here are some more classics from the Hamilton guffbank:

'And Hyypia rises like a giraffe to head the ball clear.'

George alludes to the giant African mammal renowned for its mighty leaps.

'Russia have beaten Ireland 4–2, Albania 4–1 and now Switzerland 4–1 at home. It would be a wise man who bet against them beating Georgia.'

George has always been a popular man down his local bookie's.

'What a goal. What a goal! Straight through the legs of Adams, it flew towards the roof of the net like a Wurlitzer! I mean, like a . . . howitzer.'

A Wurlitzer is a type of organ.

'We could let them score one now and they wouldn't have time to score another.'

George perhaps reveals why he chose commentary above coaching as he comes up with a novel way of running down the clock.

'Kevin Moran . . . oldest man on the pitch today . . . 35 years of age . . . of course the referee could possibly be older than that . . . and technically he's on the pitch too . . . then again his linesmen could be even older than him . . . but are they technically "on" the pitch?'

George digs and digs till daylight is but a distant memory.

George: Roy Carsley has it.

Jim Belgin: Lee Carsley, George.

George: Ah, yes, perhaps it's because his head reminds me of Ray Wilkins.

'Italy are preparing to make a substitution – and it is, the unmistakable figure . . . of Roberto Baggio.'

George announces the arrival on the pitch of . . . Gianluca Vialli. Unfortunately, the two subs had got their shirts mixed up.

'And Ireland have got to contain the brothers Baggio.'

George surely was the only one not to know.

'The Baggio brothers, of course, are not related.'

But at least he cleared it up. Or did he?

'If that's not offside, I'm a Chinaman!'

George reveals his oriental background after a perfectly correct refereeing decision.

'You, sir, are an idiot!'

George politely rebukes Lilian Laslandes after a red-card offence.

'He's pulling him off. The Spanish manager is pulling his captain off!'

Oft repeated, never quite equalled.

'Red sky at night, good day tomorrow.'

George reckons that the popular proverb needs a little simplification.

'Two–nil and the ability to score goals in seventeen consecutive matches . . . getting the ball in the net . . . it . . . the shape of what we're to expect . . . even if Iran are good . . . has to be positive.'

George in succinct stylist mode.

'And we're now watching a traditional Korean Drum Dance, performed by the appropriately named Kim Yung Bong.'

George finds something of interest during the World Cup draw preliminaries.

'We're into the second moment of stoppage time of which there isn't one.'

George breaks new ground to become the first commentator to enter a time vacuum.

'. . . the industrious Czech, to the German Hamann, to Murphy, the quintessential Englishman.'

No doubt even Danny Murphy would doff his top hat to that one.

And finally, what about George's magnificent obituary for Germany in Euro 2004:

'There was a '70s German singer called Katia Epstein. She had a song "Wenn Eine Neue Tage Bacht" – When a New Day Dawns – and one of the lines of the song referred to when the troubles of the past are being *vergessen und verbei* – forgotten and past. Well, they won't forget the European Championship but they'll want to, and it will certainly be something in the past for them!'

Whatever you say, George.

POSTSCRIPT: SPECIAL SPONSORS' AWARD

BEST QUOTE OF EURO 2004

We've averted an unpleasant showdown with the Pepsi, Gillette, Adidas, Brylcreem and Vodafone corporations with the eleventh-hour inclusion of this very special award, designed especially for the highly sponsored apple of the aforementioned corporate eyes. We didn't want a repeat of the angry scenes that occurred at the presentation of the Gaffta Player's Award, whose shock winner was not their man, but the relatively unsponsored Gazza. Conducted in the manner of a BBC Sports Personality of the Year award, we bombarded our Gaffta Panel with endless video propaganda, and then celebrated joyously when they came up trumps with the right choice. Happy now, corporate sector?

WINNER

☆David Beckham

The day of England's quarter-final with Portugal began as it ended for Becks – with an embarrassing gaffe:

Gary Newbon (ITV): David, was Wayne Rooney disappointed to lose his youngest goalscorer record on Monday to the young Swiss striker?

David Beckham: No, but I'm sure it'll just make him even more determined to get it back against Portugal tonight.

SOURCES

Since 2001, DangerHere.com has been compiling guff from around the football world.

For this book, we have also scoured the Internet for more incriminating evidence against our Gaffta contenders.

Some of these sites were:

The Rivals Network
www.rivals.net
Guardian Football
www.footballunlimited.com
The Football Quotes Page
www.geocities.com/SouthBeach/Palms/6687/quotes.html
Arseweb
www.arseweb.com
Football Quotes of the Year
www.beamused.me.uk
It's Up For Grabs Now
www.btinternet.com/~upforgrabsnow/treatment.html
Big Soccer
www.bigsoccer.com

Visit our website at www.dangerhere.com

LIST OF GAFFTA AWARDS, ALSO-RANS, NOMINEES AND WINNERS

THE GAFFERS

THE COMMENTATORS

THE CO-COMMENTATORS

THE PLAYERS

THE ANCHORS

THE PUNDITS

The Also-Rans

The Nominees

The Winner

THE RADIO COMMENTATORS

The Also-Rans

The Nominees

The Winner

THE YANKS

THE IRISH

HONOURABLE MENTIONS